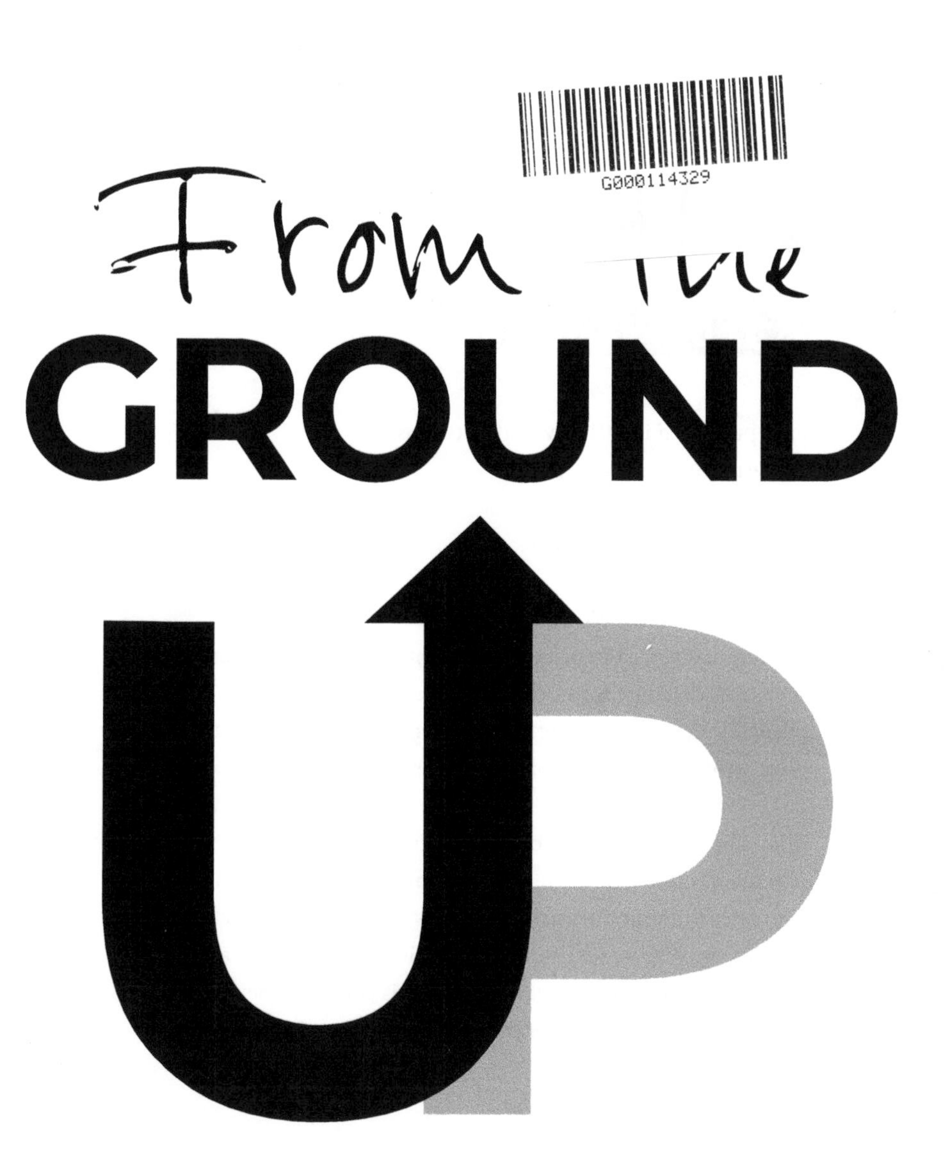

How to make marketing work hard throughout your business

LOUISE WALKER

R∃THINK PRESS

First published in 2013 by Rethink Press
(www.rethinkpress.com)

Illustrations by Louise Walker

For Eloise. You can achieve whatever you want to: be inspired, work as hard as you can and don't forget to have fun too! Love you always.

Contents

Introduction

I believe it is vital to make sure that marketing is embedded throughout any company, to enable it to grow and increase sales – both through existing and new customers.

Promoting the understanding that everyone in a business has a role to play in driving success and growth is also important, and it does not matter what their job title is – anyone working in the company is part of the marketing.

Employees will share their work experiences– good and bad – with others, and these will affect the way that the company is perceived. Getting everyone on board by sharing information and asking for feedback will lead to staff being ambassadors for the business.

When companies are in early development, they often have limited or no dedicated marketing resource, and this has the effect of limiting their growth when they reach a certain size and turnover level. It is at this point that robust, practical marketing strategies need to be in place as there will be many changes happening – getting them right is essential.

My company bridges that gap. We work with business owners to get their marketing working harder, increase sales, find talented individuals to take them further, turn opportunities they already have into cash – and work on finding new products or services that will be 'game-changers' for their businesses.

I have written this book to highlight the business and marketing areas that I believe are the main factors to focus on for growth and building long term success. I have included examples of my own experience over the past 20 years, from both working in senior corporate roles and now with my own client base.

This book is for business owners who have grown their companies successfully and are ready to grow further. By looking at what is happening inside the business, reviewing plans and implementing some (or all) of the suggestions, you will be able to make the next step in a structured way that leads to long term growth.

We have a huge amount of talent in the UK, and many outstanding businesses. Working with growing companies to make sure they have marketing strategies to achieve great success in the future is my passion. Making sure they get there is what motivates me, and seeing the results is very rewarding.

1

Look at the whole business plan

This chapter looks at the importance of making a regular and thorough review of your company's plans. By checking the plans you can avoid mistakes and shape the future. We also look at the importance of teams and communication throughout the business.

Why is it important?

In order to move forward, grow, and in some cases even survive, from a marketing viewpoint it is crucial to review the whole of your business plan regularly – and not just to look at this quarter versus last quarter versus last year, and so on.

Boards of directors can become focused on numbers as the key factor in success and growth, ignoring or side-lining the many other things inside the business which contribute to that growth, and can really drive the business forward.

How many times have you held a board meeting where the Finance Director is surrounded only by spreadsheets of figures? This is very common, not only in large businesses but also in small companies. The responsibility to shareholders and stakeholders must be met, so the numbers are vitally important.

In a regular review, every key function and business area has to present what they have been doing, but do they really all tie together? An international relocation business I worked in many years ago would start putting their presentations and board papers together several weeks before they had to present, leaving other important customer issues and business needs to drift.

This used to happen once a quarter, and probably took those key people in the business unit away from their main priorities for about a week in total.

The other sad thing about this was that this would be the first time during the quarter where the management team and functions came together, so we were really running businesses and departments in isolation from each other. None of them knew what the marketing team had been doing, and the marketing team in general did not have enough understanding of the operational part of the company. There was limited (if any) sharing of information.

Good use of time and something that would have made the process faster (and more relevant), would have been to hold weekly – or at least monthly – meetings to review the products, then setting up some smaller working parties to create different sections. If the geography would make this tricky in your business, as it was for us, a conference call would solve the issue.

This part of the business was actually very successful from a financial point of view, but could have been a game-changing business had the attitude of the management team been different.

It is vital to look at the business plan as a whole, but from all areas, not just a financial perspective or a marketing perspective and so on. It is also vital to fully involve all of the key people in the business and listen to them equally.

Avoid mistakes

When the whole plan is reviewed, it gives you the opportunity to avoid mistakes. By looking at what has happened in the past, the same mistakes can be avoided in the future. For example, if a new branch or operation has been opened in the company, it is likely that a template or format from the last (or first) branch that you opened will have been used.

Did you sit down with the whole team that opened the last branch to get their views and opinions on what could have been done better or differently? Sitting down with the team that actually opened and have run that branch is key to making sure that you learn before the next one.

If you just talk to the management team you may be missing vital input; the people 'on the ground' are as much part of the business plan and management team as the people making the strategic decisions.

Gaining feedback and insight from those involved in the day-to-day running of the business will help you to drive forward in the right direction, avoid making mistakes that will cost time and money – and also gain positive buy-in from that team.

If they are being asked their opinion it will improve morale and also foster a rounded business where everyone is involved and valued. There is a time issue – a diary that is probably too full already – but not understanding what is really going on at grass roots is a mistake that a lot of management teams make.

Reviewing the plan enables you to stop things that are not working. Putting resources, whether time, people or money, into something that is not having the right outcome for the business as a whole will not help it to move forward and grow.

I worked with a UK based scientific company who was a good example of this. They employed a sales person, gave him a computer, databases, product training and all the tools that he needed. Then they left him to get on with the job. On the surface it seemed as though he was making progress. When I came in to review the sales function nothing could have been further from the truth.

We put in place the measurement and monitoring that had been missing and this quickly gave us a picture of where the changes needed to be made. Over time, the resources that the client was putting into the sales function began to be profitable and had the effect they needed it to.

Very often, management teams will keep doing the same things year on year when in fact, if they had reviewed the whole business plan often, they would have stopped and been able to learn what is not working. That enables a change in direction or, sometimes, just not losing any more money on a plan that may have been a good idea in theory, but in practice simply has not had the expected result.

Shaping the future

Looking at your objectives enables you to see what the future will look like for the company if things are left the way they are or if they are changed.

The change might be slight or it might be huge. Maybe there is a product that is outperforming the rest and needs additional resource to grow further. It might not have had this in past years if it has not been the core or 'cash-cow' product or service.

But it is not the past that you need to look at; where can this product grow to in the future? Might it be worth investigating further to decide whether resources need to be reallocated into different areas or in different proportions?

Sometimes this may simply be the marketing budget. In many of the businesses I work with, we start to reallocate portions of money once we have reviewed the business plan and understand the direction.

Looking at the overall plan helps to make balanced and informed decisions. Every department, product or service in the business will be clamouring for additional resource at budget time; why not pre-empt that by reviewing and researching before the battle begins.

Then the influencing factors will be in place and, as a management team, you can identify where to place the resource, and the budget planning being undertaken by your teams or staff can reflect this. There will be greater clarity about the direction of the business and an understanding of what each part of the company can take. This will aid structured growth significantly.

Eliminating arguments and unproductive competition between departments or business areas in a company is one of the hardest things to achieve – and may never be totally eradicated regardless of the effort that is made.

Reviewing the business plan can help with this issue though. If there is a product or service area that has been allowed to become 'top dog', it can be very counter-productive for the growth of the business as a whole, and mean that you might lose opportunities in other areas because of the focus and strength in one product or service.

By looking at the performance of each area, you might find that the core product is not the one that needs to lead the way for the future. The market will be changing, shrinking or growing in one area, and it may be time to realign the business to really move forward.

If you give one area of the business more money than another, do they really need that to keep functioning or growing? Could you put extra cash into another area to make a better return or change the nature of the business to accelerate its growth?

When budget time comes, everyone is working towards gaining additional prizes for their departments, but are they seeking them for the right reasons? When a review of the whole plan has been made, the departments can be approached and asked to focus on an identified key area for their growth or budget request.

Similarly, this also gives you the opportunity to say that you are looking to change direction and that there will only be a certain amount of budget available. Then they can work with this rather than wasting their resource on trying to gain more where it simply will not be given.

Some businesses I have worked with allocate an amount of money, but do not assign it to anywhere specific. When they go through the budget process, they use this extra 'pot' for the best idea or business growth plan. It gets the teams motivated and rewards innovative thinking.

More effective teams

Reviewing the business plan for the company is not just about avoiding mistakes and shaping the future, though. It is also about people.

Look at the shape of the company alongside the business plan: you should understand where all the staff fit in and what each team is made up of.

Do all of the positions meet the needs of the business? You may find that you have roles that you no longer need, some that you would like to move – and talented individuals who need a challenge or promotion opportunity.

Unlocking talent should be an important part of the management team's role in the business. Many teams try and hold back people who show talent because they are afraid of the effect it may have on their own positions. Sometimes talent is simply not looked for at all; it is not seen as important or relevant. Targets and financial performance, or the day-to-day running of the business are often the sole focus.

Talent should be embraced and harnessed – there will be people in the company who can deliver much more towards the future growth of the business if they are given the right opportunity and mentoring. This also forms the basis of succession planning, vital for any business that wants to grow and move forward.

Is there a finance person connected to each business or operational area in the company? Often the finance department sits in a room of its own, sometimes not fully aware of what is happening in the rest of the company. They may see it from a number on a sheet, but it would be so much more beneficial if they were aligned to a department, product or service; that will give them a more rounded view and also help the business area they work in to improve their financial skill.

Finance is only one example of this, but looking at the whole plan will help you to identify other areas. In my experience, having a finance person involved in one of the businesses I worked in would have been hugely helpful.

I was the marketing manager for the business to business services in a large international relocation company, and our management team were always wary of giving information to finance, instead trying to keep something hidden or second-guess what they would be asked at a board review. This seemed more akin to a game of cat and mouse or bluff than a serious business.

This meant that the business area did not grow as quickly as they were capable of; they wanted to keep everything to themselves and run things their own way. In the end, through a strong CEO who could see the value in change, we had a finance person.

It took time to settle down, but once it did, the value of having them there was huge. It enabled testing of models and ideas for growth, better relationships with the board, and assistance with looking at the current business branches in more detail – helping to identify areas for growth and additional resource – and for changing the personnel structure to achieve this.

Sharing the business plan and making reviews also increases the awareness of all staff about the company. One privately owned education business I worked with recently has a really good way of doing this.

Three times a week they hold a briefing meeting for all staff, commencing before the start of the working day. Not everyone can attend, but most people are there and a set of bulleted notes are sent out to all staff after the meeting too, via email. Those not at the meeting will still receive the key points.

In the briefings, the key events are shared: prospective client visits and the areas they are interested in, information and feedback received from the board, departmental events, and so on. There is also an opportunity at the end of the briefing for staff to voice individual concerns, areas where they may need help, and progress they are making.

All departments are involved, and it is a really good way of seeing what is happening throughout the business from the top down to the bottom. I found this invaluable for assisting them with their marketing planning and strategy because it gave me a very good snapshot of where I needed to focus in the short and medium term that I would not otherwise have gained.

It was a simple way of involving everyone, ironing out issues before they arose and making sure that we all knew what was happening in the business and where we needed to put our time and effort.

In short, it was a regular review of the business plan that kept everyone on track and internal scuffles to a minimum! This business has sensitive information to share, and trust was important. The briefing sessions encouraged involvement from all staff and, through the open forum, emerging talent was also easily spotted.

Understand your direction

Who decides and how?

When you review the business plan, it cannot be in isolation. You need to look at external factors and influences that have shaped your current thinking and how they may have changed or be changing in the future.

It is likely that some parts of the plan have been inherited and others have been shaped by your team. The strategy has to come from the top – the board, CEO or business owner – but not just by looking at what you are currently doing.

Looking at the external influences that are affecting the business plan is an important part of the review. Is the market still the same as when the plan was written? Markets are changing all the time, some by a little and some by a lot.

The marketing team or staff member responsible should be involved in the business plan review. They are – or should be – at the heart of what is happening outside the company, looking at the factors that will be shaping both sales and customer growth.

Failing to involve them in the review is a big mistake. Often they are only brought out at board reviews and budget meetings, and sometimes they are occupying a shared role with another discipline. For example, one client I worked with had a marketing role shared with a health and safety role – this was how the business had grown, and not a conscious decision.

In an agency I worked for, I only went to the 'main' meetings, and although asked for input, I did not always have enough context to make the best contribution. Others were making decisions about markets that I was working in. They did not always use the resource that they were paying for properly – it could have made a big difference to the overall operation, and increased understanding within the leadership team.

Now I use my business and marketing experience to work with companies and avoid making those mistakes. Working with them to plan properly, use their existing resources effectively and take their companies to where they want them to be.

Other areas that can influence decisions about changing or moving the business objectives when you review the plan are acquisitions. Has the market changed in such a way that a merger, acquisition or a sale would make a big impact?

Sometimes, in order to grow, you have to re-group and change direction, and this is what reviewing the plan is about. Then a game-changer could be to acquire a competitor or complementary business, to sell one of your own businesses or to merge all or part of your business with another for increased market strength and dominance.

None of these options are quick or easy, but they are some of the initiatives that can come out of the business plan review as being part of the way forward.

When I worked for the relocation company, I was involved with an acquisition team to buy a competitor's business. The business owner was very shrewd and knew how to make money – having made a fortune over the years. The business we were buying was a natural fit and we wanted to purchase it to increase our share of the market.

On paper, it looked like a good investment. In reality, it tied up a lot of senior people in the business for a long time and it became apparent that the result was not going to be worth the investment. The board continued, however, and the business was bought.

The market forces at the time were not kind: a recession had begun, meaning that this particular market was shrinking due to conditions that were a result of the wider economy. The shrewdness of the owner meant that no assets were bought, we leased the assets back and that was where the real money was.

This is an example of how reviewing a business plan could have achieved a different result. A business that was achieving good performance and was very well respected in the marketplace was difficult to merge culturally, and soon lost its very experienced leader, unsettling customers, suppliers and the staff.

The results were predictable. Sales slowed, morale nose-dived and the business soon became a shadow of its former self. It never recovered.

The overall business plan review would have shown that this was not an area to invest resource in: looking at the personnel would have shown that this was a finely balanced, well run part of the business. Doing something different would have been more productive. Seriously discussing walking away from the purchase would have been sensible. There would have been a loss of money, but no sacrifice of the existing business and expertise within it.

Tell everyone

When you have reviewed the plan, it is imperative that everyone in the business knows what direction the company is taking and what the overall vision is.

It needs to be communicated internally in as many ways as possible. All your staff are marketing the business every single day and they need to be ambassadors spreading positive news.

The most effective way to do this is to be transparent, not just keeping the strategy and objectives of the business in the senior management team (except where there may be confidential issues); spread the word in the right way and everyone will feel involved and more positive about what their company is doing.

About 20 years ago this would largely have been carried out, if at all, by a memo pinned to an ageing noticeboard. Those days are largely over, and there are also many other new ways in which to communicate with staff and teams.

The key component of communication is to make sure that you are sending the message out in a way that it will be received and digested by everyone in the company. Using one form of communication will not work for everyone.

Think about your audience: you need to speak to them in a language that they will understand, and part of that could be to deliver the message through people in the business who have credibility. Staff are more likely to respond positively if they hear news from someone that they respect, like and trust.

Engage the marketing team in visiting every layer of the business; they will then be able to put together several communication pieces that will talk to each different department in the company, in the right language and medium.

Using the company intranet, noticeboards, staff briefings and any other communication channel that already exists is important. Video footage of the senior team or CEO explaining what is happening at regular intervals – for example monthly – will also mean that the business appears to be transparent from the top down.

This will create buy-in and increase awareness in your team at every level of the business. The staff will want to share the message that could lead to new clients, and it will certainly lead to an improvement in customer service and morale.

A large international corporate I worked in had the opposite approach for many years. Keeping the team away from what was happening and the direction that the business was taking caused resentment. This in turn had a negative impact on the attitude of staff – particularly those at the front line serving our customers.

As this then translated to the experience that the customers received and travelled upward, the teams became more difficult to manage and felt totally separated from the senior management. This was recognised and solved through a new set of processes and a restructure. A positive outcome was achieved by making changes and having regular reviews.

By being more open, the businesses I work with now are able to make big improvements and create a good team ethic that also helps them to identify talent. Staff will naturally come forward wanting to do more or improve their role and career when they feel valued.

Lean into it

Once you have reviewed the plan, whether changing significantly or remaining largely the same, you need to get behind it fully. Communicating effectively to your team plays a major role in this, and the senior management also need to be giving the same message.

The company has a direction. It will probably change again as the business grows, trying different things and tweaking the strategy – but there is a clear path to follow.

One of my more recent clients is a project management company and has entered a market with a service that is not well understood, but delivers a huge amount of value once the client does understand it and can see the results. This service delivers value to homeowners who are having building or extension works carried out, and means that they only have one contractor to work with rather than several. They knew on entering the market that it was going to be as much about education as about sales.

They had made the decision that there was a place for their service and then built a business plan to achieve their objectives. Even when things were not going well, they kept driving forward because they had a conviction that it would work.

They leaned into the plan and embraced it. They are so passionate about the value that they deliver and the savings they can make for their clients that people started to believe in it too. ClearPlan Project Management grew from a base in their home with just the two of them; they now have two regional business awards and staff working for them, along with many ambassadors through the networking and hard work that they have put in.

This is because the plan that they had was communicated continuously from the top of their company to everyone that they met, and to their prospective clients. They got behind the plan and reviewed it regularly to make sure they were on the right path, making changes when they needed to, and seeking feedback and guidance in specialist areas.

Know your history

Reviewing the business plan is also about looking backwards. This may seem strange, but knowing where and how the current plans for the business have been developed makes a huge difference to how the company moves forward.

Look at how the company has developed. Has it been shaped by market forces, competitors or products and services? For most companies, large or small, it will have been a combination of all of these things and maybe some other factors too.

Now it is time to shape the future of the business on your terms. Market forces and competitors can be affected by looking at how the company has operated in the past and spotting opportunities from this to move forward – or maybe even change the company's game plan completely.

Is the business still the same as it was two years ago? Recently we have experienced a double-dip recession in the UK, coupled with recession in the USA and across Europe. All of these things will have changed the market forces to a certain extent.

By looking back, an approach could be found that has been tried before and not worked, but the timing and market conditions might mean that it will work now.

What has worked in the past should not be left on a shelf or dismissed because it is not 'modern' or because it was someone else's idea. These things can gain more clients for the company and should be investigated.

When the relocation company I worked for launched a document storage business as a standalone service, the main company had already been selling this in pockets as an additional revenue generator, for many years through the core business. One of the marketing activities that they had been carrying out to generate sales was to send out a flat archive storage box with a sales letter to local businesses.

I came across this idea when I visited a branch in Scotland for a meeting about something entirely different, but nobody in the newly launched standalone service had gathered any information about what had worked in the past.

I used this method and it had some really good results. It was inexpensive, but made a statement because the flat box was large and could not be ignored by the recipient! Even if they did not become a client, the box with our branding would be used and so it, in effect, became an ambassador for us.

This shows that looking backwards was a positive step to take. We were able to use ideas that had worked in the past to generate business now and in the future.

How much has changed?

When a company looks backwards, it will also see how much has changed, both inside the business and outside. Different services may be offered now, or there may be a change in emphasis on where the main revenue steam lies.

Seeing what has changed will help with looking at what you want to achieve in the future, becoming focused on the market forces and opportunities that are there to take.

If the products and services have all been offered and delivered offline, is there a way or a value to be had in delivering some of them online? The internet and technology has grown very quickly over the last 10 years, customer buying patterns have changed and so have their needs and expectations.

It may be that internal communications or processes can change to become more effective and efficient. Looking backwards will provide the information to help inform decision making now. Revenues may have come predominantly from one area – can you make a change to create new revenue from the existing area but in a different way?

My business has changed since it began over eight years ago. I did not use the internet to sell services or generate income, I used face-to-face networking to first establish and then grow my client base. By looking back at my business plan, I recognised that I needed to make some changes and use web-based services more effectively to generate income and raise the profile of the company.

I implemented a new service that could be bought by any business to give them advice about their marketing, anywhere in the world. Previously, all of my clients had been in a fixed geographical radius from my office base; now they can get marketing advice and support wherever they are.

If I had not looked back at my plan and where my history had been, I would not have been able to spot this service quickly. Knowing my history enabled me to determine where the future should be and has shaped my own planning, enabling me to establish new services and client locations.

Summary

- Review plans regularly and challenge them
- Remove or change activities that are not gaining results
- Make sure that staff are in the right roles
- Communicate with everyone in the business effectively
- Look backwards – understand the history of the company

2

Review your current plans

In this chapter we focus on the shorter-term plans and the need for involving staff and gaining feedback. We also look at the importance of marketing and the need to have a consistent style of presentation to enable comparisons to be made easily.

It's not just about the numbers

Reviewing the whole company business plan is important, and equally important is a regular review of the current shorter-term plans and activity.

The numbers are important, they are the marker for the financial performance of the company and need to be focused on to ensure that the business is on track and to understand the areas where assistance and improvement need to be made.

The finance team should not only be focused on the numbers, though; they tell one side of the business, but there are other factors too. Apart from the Finance Director – and a very good one is essential – does the finance team understand what the business actually does? They should be working with the business units to help them understand finance and to improve their knowledge of the products and services, and the operational delivery of them.

When a finance team is integrated into the business, issues get dealt with quickly and the team is working together for growth, rather than against each other for the right numbers result.

An international events company I worked for had the entire finance team in a closed-off room with a security panel on the door. I could not enter unless they opened the door for me and, as a board director, I found it quite strange that they were so separated from the rest of the company.

They saw the rest of the company as 'being against' them because they were isolated and had a locked door between them and the business. This did not help productivity or attitude on either side.

Issues were slow to be dealt with and it was difficult to understand what was happening with the company's finances, except through a quarterly review. With the exception of the Finance Director, the finance team in return did not understand the impact of their role on the daily operation of the company.

A well-run business integrates this team; this then enables them to add value through their skill and experience.

There are no surprises at board meetings when the finance team is integrated in the business, and opportunities for growth often arise too. An understanding of why things happen in a certain way and an appreciation of what the company sells or makes is crucial for the growth and success of the business as a whole.

The team in the business benefit greatly by learning from the finance team. They have an appreciation of what is behind the numbers, why and how targets are set and budgets allocated. Performance can be improved significantly by working together and holding a collective responsibility for the growth of their area.

Where to grow

Another important aspect of reviewing the current plans, not related to the numbers, is growth. Looking at what is happening allows you to drill down into specific areas of the business or in a team.

This helps with growth. Gaps in skill or experience within a team or unit may be impeding its performance. One team may be very strong and doing very well: this gives you the opportunity to use them as a template for recruiting and benchmarking against.

Addressing issues in business areas is easier if the current strategy is reviewed regularly, not just at the board meeting. If you are meeting resistance from one area of a team, it is easily spotted when looking at what is happening currently.

Then there is the opportunity to solve the issue rather than it being left to cause additional damage until the formal review happens.

Of course, a team will be in place to ensure that this happens, but a good CEO will be aware of what is going on in the business and will be looking at how to enhance and improve things for the stakeholders. It is up to the senior management team to make sure that the right people are in place and to create a structure that maximises the potential for growth – beyond the strategy.

Often, a senior individual will be able to create a dominant position that is counter-productive in the business. This individual can take up a lot of management time and have a big influence over other team members in their own area – and sometimes in the whole company.

I have seen this happen several times, and it has never ended well. Through constant review, this situation can sometimes be avoided, and a plan put in place to deal with it. If the individual has key knowledge or a skill that is seen as vital to the business, the senior team need to look at succession-planning, enabling them to water down the dominance by approaching it from a different angle.

Monitoring gives control back to the CEO and decision makers. It has to happen as there is a significant risk of negative impact on the performance of the company and the staff if it is not recognised and dealt with.

Whole company awareness

Another area that makes an important point for continuous review are the voices coming from within the company: the employees.

A good business will be talking to and listening to their staff, at all levels of the organisation.

This involves several functions in the company. Human Resources personnel are really well placed to be informative about members of staff, their performance, and finding hidden talent in the business.

Charge them with looking at the people, not as sheets of paper or files, but as individuals. Look at the appraisal system: does the current process help to find the people who want to go further; or those who have useful skills that could be developed and make a difference to the growth and direction?

There are many different appraisal systems that can be used by a business to evaluate and develop staff performance, set objectives and measure results. Make sure that the system being used also allows managers and appraisers to put forward talented individuals for growth and succession-planning.

There may be issues within a business unit that are affecting the team performance. This may not come to light by just looking at the numbers during a review. Have one of the HR personnel linked to each business unit as part of their responsibilities, and they will uncover any issues like these. Or, if the HR department is one person, get them talking to each area or member of the team: this will produce the same result.

If there is no dedicated HR team, or this is a role that is shared with another discipline, think about getting some outside advice and review the people who are working in the company.

In the events business I worked in, we had one person with both HR and Health and Safety responsibility. The business had a lot of equipment and staff, and Health and Safety was a very important and dominant operational issue. This meant that most of his time was taken up on non-HR issues, which in turn meant that a lot of HR problems were stacking up and not being dealt with quickly.

Because of the many changes in the legal system relating to employees, senior managers were either dealing with situations and mis-managing them, leading to the company being involved in legal proceedings, or simply not dealing with them and allowing them to fester – developing into much larger complications that directly affected the growth of the company.

Having an awareness of the whole business as part of these regular reviews means that simple issues can be addressed, giving some quick wins and improving or maintaining morale. For example, maybe the coffee machines need replacing or the communal staff areas need redecorating: these are both easy things to change with little cost involved, but will make the staff feel cared for and listened to.

The main point here is that there should be a review with all functions and not just the business areas and financial position.

Marketing process

When you hold a review, whether it is monthly or quarterly, how is your marketing represented? In some businesses it is a separate function under the management of a marketing director or member of the senior management team; in others it may be aligned with the business areas that they are marketing. It can also be a shared role with another discipline, or no internal role at all.

Regardless of where the marketing team or person sits within the business, they are a crucial part of the review process and need to be utilised effectively for the growth and development of the company.

I worked in a relocation company where my role and team were aligned to the businesses that I was working with. I had to prepare for quarterly reviews with each unit, and this was usually when I found out what was really happening and the direction that we were working towards.

At that time, the company did not see marketing as important enough to share the direction with. I was quite removed from the planning and operations and wheeled out as part of the team only on these occasions.

Obviously, this did not help the business areas I worked in. The value that they were missing was the skill that I had in my role to be able to give advice and make improvements to the direction, and to challenge some of the thinking from a marketing perspective.

Numbers were seen as key; marketing was seen as non-crucial. This can be the case in organisations and it is a reason why they do not grow.

Marketing should be at the heart of every company, not just in the marketing department, but across all functions. The reason for having a marketing person should be to use their skills to take the business in the right direction, understanding customer needs and buying patterns, where they may be changing, and keeping the company ahead.

Give the marketing people a set of directions to follow: they should be involved with the business they work in and have a good understanding of everything that is going on. Letting the business management team operate without involving marketing until review time will not assist good growth results.

The research from the marketing team may not always fit

directly with the numbers and should be a source of challenge and debate. They should be engaged and reporting on the following areas as a matter of course.

The economic climate - looking at markets that directly affect the company

This should be the market or markets that clients are in and the countries that the business operates in as well as the overall country economy. All of these things have a bearing on where growth will come from and identify any new areas that may not have been considered. It will also assist with identifying early when customers may start to buy less, why, and for how long.

The UK was going into a decline in manufacturing when I was working in the industrial business. This could have put the business in jeopardy as many of our traditional customers were scaling down operations. However, in the short term, this meant more business for us as we worked with them to downsize and move locations, while we worked out how to adapt to the longer-term situation.

At the time, China was emerging as a fast growing economy and it was also cheaper to produce goods abroad in some European countries. Recognising this early meant that we were able to focus on these areas and gain business from a new set of customers. What affected one set of core clients was not the same for the newly emerging clients. That helped the business to remain both stable and to grow.

Budget – the plans that were written at budget time may need to be changed

The marketing team should be constantly reviewing their budget and areas for spend to ensure that the money is being invested in the right places. This is necessary both for sustaining the current customer base, and proposing areas for change based on research, or any changes in the market.

Do some of the spend areas need to change, or budget allocation increase, if one business unit has more opportunity than another? A good Finance Director will certainly be aware of the whole picture and will be highlighting areas where budget can be moved to give a greater return.

This is where regular review, with the right questions, is invaluable. If the business has one product or service and one marketing person or team, the advice is the same.

Looking at the markets in which clients operate and the changes and forces within those markets is crucial for the business. In fact, it could be argued that it is even more crucial if the company is operating in one market only, or providing just one product or service.

You may need to attract more clients who are smaller in revenue, or fewer clients who provide a larger return for you. In reality, a mixture of both is usually necessary.

The other important factor to remember about reviews is that issues or key information that arise between them should not wait until the next review to be aired. The quicker everyone is aware of influencing factors, the better equipped the business is to deal with them before they become an adverse reality.

Compare like for like

One of the things that I have always found surprising in corporate reviews is the difference between the presentation of one business against another.

There are some financial sections that will be reported in the same way for all of the business areas, and that enables the Finance Director, CEO and senior management teams to compare them equally, against each other, with few modifications.

The rest of the presentation given by each business or function is often left up to them, both in style and content.

If the presentation templates are streamlined, it will create a focused approach and allow comparison in the performance of different functions within each business unit, like for like. This will also give better visibility of the return being made on investment in areas like marketing that can often be difficult to directly quantify.

The personalities of the people in each area will still give a different style of presentation, but overall you will create a much less 'maverick' approach to the presentations being seen each time there is a review. The team in the business will also be able to see the effect of marketing and sales spend (for example) directly, and then are in a better position to make informed judgements about where to focus activity.

When the information is displayed in the same way each time, the gaps can be seen and the right questions can be asked. This will show what is working and where there may need to be changes or adjustments made. Some activities will not be directly measurable – an exhibition for example, but they may be activities that are necessary for brand awareness or showing strength and position in your marketplace or industry.

When I managed the marketing function for four different business to business services involved in relocation of offices, industrial plant and document management, I presented at many reviews. Each management team had a different style of presentation and I wanted to find a way to compare what I was achieving in one business versus another. I created a marketing template that allowed me to present the budget, activity and measurement in the same way for each business so that I (and the board) could understand the effect across the B2B platforms, making changes or combining activities where there was a benefit.

It gave clarity to my team and also to the senior management who could now compare the marketing function across the businesses more easily, instead of the scattergun approach that had been used previously.

In the template presentation, allow one 'free' section where each team can present new ideas. This will begin to drive creativity and encourage them to think about new ways to drive their area and increase their growth.

Having an 'innovation' section can provide new ideas that might influence the overall business plan, and also identify talented individuals who are challenging the current thinking.

The team running the business areas everyday know their market and the customers they are serving. They are best placed to come up with new ideas if they are given the freedom to do this in a safe environment, where the finance team can then look more closely at whether the idea is viable either now or in the future.

Summary

- The business is about more than just the balance sheet
- Integrating finance with business areas is important
- Engage with staff at all levels to gain feedback
- Have marketing at the heart of the company
- Create consistent presentation styles

▸3

Know your customers – and how to serve them

Having an in depth profile of your target clients is vital. By looking at how to achieve this, and all aspects of customers past, present and future, you can make the right decisions about where to focus in order to create strong growth. This chapter looks at all things 'customer'.

Build a profile

The best way to start the process of really understanding who your customers are, why they buy from you now, and what kind of customers you want (or need) for the future is to build a profile.

Looking at your current customer base and researching is important, but this stage should come second. If this is carried out first, it is likely that the thinking will be influenced by what exists already and not what it is that the business really needs.

What do your ideal customers look like?

It is amazing the effect that building a profile of a customer(s) can have on the business growth and the effectiveness of the marketing activity.

Begin with the demographics. This is not an exhaustive list, but the analysis should include:

- How old are they?
- What gender are they?
- Where do they live?
- Where do they work?
- What job role do they have?
- How much do they earn?
- What size is their business?

- Which market or industry are they in?
- What is their turnover?
- How many employees do they have?

Some of the items on this list will not apply to every business, but by using the ones that do, a comprehensive, demographic profile can be completed. The next stage is to build a psychological profile. The psychological profile will enable you to determine the type of person or business that the company wants to have as a customer.

Again, these points are not definitive, but will provide a basis for thought and to begin the process. Consider:

- Influential – industry leader?
- Successful – growing or established?
- Decision maker – can they make purchasing decisions?
- Innovative – challenging, open to ideas, try new services or products?
- Profile – high profile in their marketplace/social media?
- Ethos – does their ethos and vision match yours?
- Environment – are environmental issues important to them or you?
- Complementary – can you partner or JV with them to grow?
- Technology – how do they use it?
- Modern – are they in tune with modern approaches to business, e.g. social media usage?

Using the points above for both demographics and psychology – and other factors that are relevant to your strategy – will deliver a target customer profile. This can then be used as a template to analyse the current client base from and map out the future.

Two of my clients have created well-defined customer profiles recently. In both cases, this has enabled them to look at their marketing activity and communications strategy to deliver targeted messages to the right prospective customers for their business.

They have been able to understand who they should be reaching and used the profile to do this. Clearly identifying their target customer has meant that they can focus on one section of their market, creating a niche and a specialism instead of the mass targeting approach they had previously used.

One client is an Independent UK insurance broker who provides insurance for high net worth individuals as part of their portfolio. By profiling their target client effectively we have been able to market specifically to them and exclude those people who would not want to look at this service. The main customers are male, aged 45+ who own their own homes and have a high income. They live in certain high value locations, and this was part of our criteria too.

The other client is a flooring specialist. They had been using social media in a scattergun way to try and attract business. Whilst this has seen some success, the targeted approach has increased that. We now seek to contact and connect with companies and individuals who fit the profile created; this is another example of accurate customer profiling that works well.

Creating a customer profile means that targeting is more defined and more effective. There is less waste as the marketing budget can be used for a clear purpose with structure that sits with the overall business plan.

Using the profiling, a specific offering can be put together that clearly meets the issues of the target market or industry, leading to an improvement in client retention and a sound basis for driving the company forward.

How do these customers behave?

Now that the type of customer you want to sell to has been established, their behaviour should be looked at in several different areas.

What are their buying patterns? When looking at the current client base and comparing it with the profile built, you will probably find that there are one or more customers who have the attributes to fit with the new profile.

Analysing their buying patterns will then show what the drivers and triggers are for purchasing. It may be that a new service or product was offered proactively, or that they came to you with an increased need for the services that they already buy.

Identifying the buying patterns of existing customers, and those you want as customers, is really important for achieving structured growth in the business. It is vital to know whether customers will be price-driven or service-driven, for example.

If price is the key factor, the team must be aware of what the market is doing and the markets that influence the clients/customers. This has to be a key area of focus for the marketing operation where price is the highest priority.

Some businesses are also seasonal or have other market influences, allowing fluctuation in price led by supply and demand. Ensuring that these patterns are identified in the business plan, along with the customer profile, will make for effective highly targeted marketing.

If the prospective customers are more service-driven than price-led, ensure that the effort goes into having strong processes in place to maintain service levels and be seen to be constantly striving to improve them.

It may be that value can be added to your customers by creating new systems to make it easier for them to interact with the company and to provide updates.

A growing part of the relocation business I worked in was during the push on PFI (Private Finance Initiative) projects. PFI's are a partnership between a public sector organisation (like a local council) and private sector companies. The private companies will make the capital investment and then recoup their money over a long period of time (sometimes 30 years) from the public sector body. This has been a popular way for new public facilities to be built, and sometimes also attracts central government investment. By their nature, these were complex relocations, mainly involving hospitals, where we built a reputation for service delivery. To add further value, we created an internet portal on our website so that all the project documentation could be kept in one place, easy to access for the client, and a demonstration of the added value that we offered during these projects.

These clients were driven on price – but equally on service as we were relocating intensive care units and other specialist and critical hospital departments where there was no margin for error.

The addition to the website gave a perceived increase in service level, but in a very simple way, at a low cost to the business, but a high value to the client.

Have you or your customers changed?

Like any relationship, the client and supplier will change over time. As the company grows, the service offering will change; as the clients grow, their needs will shift. Keeping track of these changes by having good communications will enable growth to happen alongside the customer, or to change direction.

Again, having a high awareness of the company's own industry and both the markets that customers operate in and are influenced by is crucial. As we have gone through a fluctuating economy and recessions in the UK, all customers will have been affected by it in some way. Recognising this, any shift in what they are buying and the frequency of purchase will enhance the competitive edge.

There may also be some opportunities for additional sales to be gained from the existing customer base, from another arm of the business or by increasing the volume or nature of the services or products provided to them already.

One of the ways that I have seen this created effectively in the past is to put an 'implant' team into large customer premises. An implant team is made up of staff who carry out specific duties or have a certain skill set that is needed by a customer. In the events company I worked for we had a specialist production team based in a London venue to set up and manage all their conferences, awards evenings and weddings. This helped to streamline the services we provided for them, and enabled the customer to have these services and the expertise of our staff on their site – improving efficiency and communication.

The added benefit of this to our business was that we had eyes and ears in our clients' business every day. We had good communication channels with our staff and were able to spot opportunities for additional sales easily, as well as increasing our service levels for those clients.

Meeting with your clients regularly also allows engagement with them about their business plans. They may be entering new markets that could mean additional sales, or changing direction that enables thought to be given about new services that could be offered, again increasing revenue and providing added value.

An existing client is often not aware of everything that your company offers. This is often the case in a multi-discipline company where a client buys one product or service, unaware that there are other services they may be interested in.

It is not up to the customer to find out about all of the services the business can offer them, but the business' responsibility to tell them. Think about giving them a short presentation of your whole offering when you meet them for a review, or invite them in with other clients to meet personnel from different areas of the company.

There are many ways to make them aware – and this could increase revenue at a much lower cost than acquiring a new client would.

Do some research

Now that you have built the ideal customer profile and looked at their behaviour, as well as any changes that you – or they – have gone through, it is time to analyse the current client base.

The database is the place to begin. Are all your clients in one place? Even if there are different levels of access for different business units or individuals, it is very important to have a central database of clients, prospects and ex-clients.

The software chosen will be driven by the type of company you have and the sales and marketing methods used. Some businesses use packages that can be bought off-the-shelf; others use a bespoke system designed for their requirements.

Over the last 20 years I have seen many different systems and worked in lots of businesses where the importance of sharing information was not recognised. The impact of being able to view everything in one place is huge. The ability to look at customers who buy from one division and not another, will lead to additional sales opportunities.

If client data is not all in one place, I would strongly encourage working towards getting it there. It will be worth the effort. The business will be able to see where there are sales synergies for upselling, and start to move out clients who are more effort than profit or who do not fit with the new customer profile. Of course, this will happen over time and not immediately, but the process can begin.

The other areas that need interrogation are prospects and therefore pipeline, lost and 'lapsed' customers.

The company needs to be aware of how many prospective clients are in the business pipeline, and the sales stage each of them are at. This is important for forecasting and growth, and also for making informed decisions on where to spend budget – as well as spotting the talented individuals who are leading the way in the sales team.

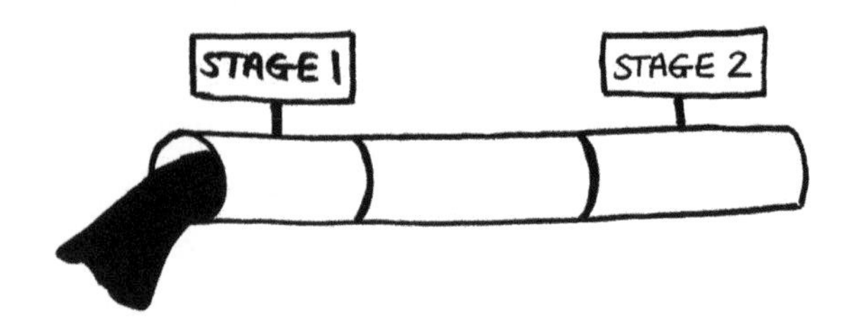

Take out those prospects that are just taking up space on the system. Get each business team to look in detail at their prospects and make a decision on whether to keep them in the system or take them out. The database needs to be as accurate as possible, not just filled with names and contacts who will never be customers.

While going through this process, the database will need to be cleansed. This will remove any businesses that are no longer trading, update details of businesses which have relocated, de-duplicate any double entries that exist, merge clients with several contacts who have been entered separately, and ultimately result in a database that is in the best possible condition of accuracy.

The database must also be checked against the TPS (Telephone Preference Service) regularly to ensure that a business that has registered its demand for no sales contact is not being called. Fines are in place for calling TPS registered businesses or consumers. Now there is a database that is completely visible, giving a picture of the entire client base across the company.

Putting this together with the customer profile, you will now be able to see if there are any existing clients with the same features. These are the clients who need to be nurtured to help the growth of the business.

Another important task that can now be undertaken is to supplement the database with new leads, by buying in data that matches your customer profile criteria exactly. This should be a key marketing focus.

Meet current clients

Current clients hold the key to the future and planning. It is important to know what they want, what their influences are, and how these might change over time. Before starting to meet them and gain feedback, clear business objectives are needed to confirm what the desired outcome is from the meetings.

Meetings need to happen in several different layers of each company. The CEO and Finance Director need to meet with their counterparts in client organisations, and so on down through the layers.

A range of meeting types should take place. Seeing clients at their premises will give information about their personalities and their business, in a place where they feel relaxed.

Invite clients to your premises. If your company has a facility that is interesting, give them a tour. Introduce them to other members of the team in different functions and parts of the business, and showcase your business to them. Use the opportunity to re-market to them.

If there are clients with obvious synergies, inviting several of them to a meeting or lunch, or putting on a seminar, speaker or event that would interest them is also a good demonstration of the awareness of their needs and your company's customer service values. Connecting key clients together can create a powerful networking opportunity – both for them and for the business.

Clients meeting other clients gives a very strong impression of the business and customer base.

Make sure that a range of staff meet them – if they have a day-to-day point of contact in the business, let them put a face to a name. It should not just be sales, account management and senior management staff involved. The more layers of the business that can be deconstructed at an event like this, the more open you will appear as an organisation.

These might seem like 'over the top' notions, but they send a powerful message to customers and will enhance relationships and therefore increase sales potential.

Establish their needs - now and future

The current customer base can provide the business with an amazing amount of information that enables you to serve them better, also allowing areas for growth and opportunity to be considered.

Talking to them and meeting them, as well as analysing the data that is held on each customer and building on the profile created, identifies the layers that make up each client. From market forces to changes in direction, evaluation of where the company sits within the relationship is a key part of growth and review.

There may be a need to make an acquisition or merge a business unit with an external company to provide complementary services. Once all the information is gathered, an informed decision can be made – once again, one that reflects the business plan, or maybe changes it.

What you are really discovering here is how you can make the best decisions for the future business growth.

Customers gain peace of mind when they feel they are being well looked after; this makes them more likely to remain a customer and also more receptive to additional sales. Most importantly, engaging customers' opinions and thoughts provides feedback that helps you improve and, at a basic level, it shows them that the company cares.

Might the customers change? In the same way that you look at growing your company, reviewing and setting targets and objectives, so too will they. Communicating with them will provide a better understanding of what is happening in their business, what is changing and what then may affect the company.

Poll the target market

Using the customer profile, select some of the current clients who share the same profile as the target clients and use them to carry out some polling.

Polling your target market will supply information about whether they are the right customers to be pursuing. Engage some external help and expertise if it is needed –it is very important to get this right. There are many different research methods depending on the budget you have available and the nature of information you need to assimilate.

Firstly, establish what it is that you need to know. Make a list of questions based on the customer research already carried out, and the business plan. These questions then need to be posed – using whichever method chosen – to the matching existing clients.

Analyse the returned data and use it as part of the decision-making process. At this point, it should be shared with everyone in the business too, to make it easier for them to help with the marketing effort.

Do not let the data stay in the marketing team. Although it may not seem relevant to the finance function because some of it will be qualitative, it is a significant part of any decision you make about implementation. They need to see it and balance it against the numbers to make good recommendations soundly based on all of the facts.

Why do they buy?

What is it about your products and services that make your customers choose to buy from you rather than from a competitor? Yours will not be the only business to offer the service they need, so what is it about your company that stands out?

The same question is equally important in reverse: you need to establish what makes potential customers *not* buy from your company. Many businesses do not analyse 'lapsed' or 'lost' customers and prospects. This is an area where you can really learn about the business and make changes.

A 'lapsed' customer may not have been looked after well enough, or had a better price from a competitor. Unless the business speaks to them to find out why they have left, a big piece of information is missing that can be used to ensure that fewer clients leave in the future.

The same applies to a prospect who signed with someone else. What was it about their service that made them choose a competitor? Purchasing decisions are not made solely on price: customers have to know you, like you and trust you as well, and it is a combination of these that influences the sale, whether consciously or unconsciously.

Service levels

Another important piece of business information that contributes to the overall plan is the customer service process: having a robust set of performance indicators in place to ensure objectives are being met – and exceeded.

It should be reviewed on a regular basis to ensure that the measurement criteria are relevant to the service offering and customer expectations. If it does not meet the criteria, change it. Quite often, staff have bonus incentives for meeting service levels and KPI targets. If these targets are not challenging enough or not meeting the customer needs, the business could be giving profit to staff who have not truly earned it.

If there are no customer complaints, does that mean that all the customers are happy and satisfied, or over-satisfied, with the work being carried out for them. They probably feel 'okay', but unless there is a proactive process for communicating with all of them, you simply will not know.

When the customer service plan is reviewed, involve your customers directly by asking for their comments on what is currently measured and delivered. This will make the customer feel valued, providing another reason to get in touch and gather feedback. Continuous feedback is vital; it gives knowledge about where you are getting things right and where improvements or changes should be made.

Customers will be able to see the value in the service process if they have been consulted about it, and it will mean relevant objective-setting and measurement in the company. Make it easy for them to see and use the information being assimilated: think about introducing a 'customer' area on the company website, for instance, where they can log in and see their own service information.

One of the businesses I used to run with a partner was an SMS platform – a simple way for companies to upload their client database and communicate with them through any (and all) of the electronic marketing channels, separately or together. In this business we had a 'client dashboard' so that our customers could easily see their services on a constantly updated basis.

It meant they could see all their activity and analyse results, transactions and so on. The visibility is a standard part of the service offering in this type of business: nothing is hidden, we want them to see the value and benefit, and be able to challenge us to improve both the service and their understanding.

Pricing

How often do you market test your pricing? When the business plan is reviewed and there is an improvement your customer knowledge, looking at the prices services and products are sold at is an important part of the work.

Take a set of services or products and put the price charged against them. Then, go out to the competition and find out what they are charging for the same services. You need to know that you are competitive on pricing and have a regular 'shopping basket' checking process in place.

This ensures that the company is in the right place for pitching services to new clients. If the pricing is higher than the competitors' you need to look at the reasons behind it. Do you have higher fixed costs and is there a way to maintain the higher price for a good reason? Maybe your costs are higher, but the level of service you provide is also much higher than the competition's.

If customers and prospective profiled customers are driven by service, then the pricing structure you have can be maintained. If they are driven by price, look at the operation behind the service and begin to work on how it can be streamlined to meet a price that the customer is willing to pay, and where a profit can still be made.

Do not undersell. If the product or service is fairly priced and has value attached, be strong. You can be a leader in a niche market, or known for having a luxury service that is aspirational to some customers and an absolute 'must-have' to others who are at that end of their own marketplace.

It is important to value the company's products and services – giving something away will not make your customer think very highly of the product. You must place a value on it in your business to ensure that the customer believes it will have value.

I have a client in the scientific sector whose business is service-based, but they had also invested in a product that removes allergens from the air and was complementary to the services they already provided. In order to start selling the product, they decided that it needed to be piloted with some customers first, to gain credibility and endorsement.

The product was already being sold in America, and it did have a very demonstrable track record. The UK company started to 'loan' these machines to their customers in the hope that once they had seen the trial results for themselves they would purchase the unit.

The problem was that by loaning them out free of charge (which also cost them time and money in installation, testing and maintenance), the customers were happy to have the units but did not feel the need to purchase them because they were getting great results for nothing!

The customers just kept extending the trial period. The first change I made to my client's business model was to charge for the trial period. The customers were then parting with money (and gaining benefit), and my client had placed a value on their product. Sales of the units increased as a result: a simple change, but a valuable one for my client's credibility – and profit margin.

This is a good example of why a value needs to be placed on what the company is selling. If the company does not seem to value its products and services, neither will the customers or prospective customers.

Products and Services

How can the company ensure that its products and services are relevant in today's market and will still be relevant and profitable tomorrow? Look ahead and make sure that the business is 'future-proof'.

To do this, you need to look at what the company is offering now, and how the markets and customers you are working with may change going forward. Technology is a key factor in this process. Can the business use technology to improve services, or change the way that it communicates or reports to customers?

Look at what the competition is doing to enhance their service offering. In the relocation business I worked in, we developed a 'client login' area on our website to enable one distinct set of customers to interact with us, and have all the information – a large part of this was spread sheets and plans – in front of them wherever they were.

This was actually too far ahead of its time. Today such tools are commonplace and standard, but at the time we developed it, the clients were not yet able to make the best use of it. This is an example of future-proofing and added value, but we should have gone back one step with the process at this point. If we had used the technology about two years later it would have been embraced more fully as it was out of its infancy and becoming mainstream, easier to use and cheaper to implement.

The other issue with the development was that our staff did not really grasp the concept well enough to be able to either use it themselves or sell it in as an additional area of added value. A lesson learned in making sure that all the business is involved in developing new services and the marketing of them is happening throughout the business and not just in the marketing department.

It may be time to invest in new skills and expertise. Technology and marketing have changed and evolved rapidly. Ensuring that the right personnel who understand these changes and can harness them to a positive effect for the business are in place, is vitally important.

This does not just involve looking at what competitors are doing, but also communicating with customers. Their marketplaces and industries will be changing as well, and their future objectives might be very different from those that they are working towards today.

Now may also be the time to look at productising for the company. Within the current range of services, determine whether some of them can be formed into products to either give to prospective customers or sell to them at a low cost. This is a way of gaining new clients, as they will be drawn into the business in stages, without necessarily asking them to make a large value purchase in the first instance.

In my business, 'productising' means writing a book to add value to the customers I work with now, and to give advice to the customers I want to work with in the future. Additionally it means looking at the services I provide now and seeing how I can make them accessible in small chunks to develop relationships with the people I want to work with.

That may be holding workshops, short or long courses and speaking about the importance of marketing being carried out through every department in a company.

By working through the process of knowing who your current customers are, building a profile for the ones you want in the future and looking at all of their needs, it will become easier to pinpoint parts of the company's offering that can be turned into products. This will lead to gaining additional business and improving visibility and credibility in your industry.

Summary

- Build a profile for each of your target customer groups
- Meet regularly with your clients
- Analyse your database
- Understand what your customers need
- Test your products, services and pricing

4

Involve all functions

As a company grows, the number of staff and business areas increase. This chapter focuses on the importance of involving people from all areas of the business and looks at the extra value that can be achieved as a result.

Why is it important?

A whole, focused approach

Involving all the departments, functions and business units gives a company a huge advantage in their marketplace. When parts of the business are left to operate alone, the maximum amount of benefit achieved will be less than if they work together in some areas.

Having a whole company approach gives a better image and increases credibility in both current and future markets. The company will not look disparate and it will provide an increased belief when pitching and presenting to customers and prospects.

It will also attract more valuable clients, as they will be able to see the whole service offering you provide, giving your company a competitive edge.

Involving people from all strands of the company also improves marketing and the ability to both cross-sell and up-sell. The team will be in a better position to spot opportunities that are not necessarily in their own areas – leading to sales that would otherwise not happen.

There is also the issue of succession planning. This is often overlooked in companies, but is vitally important for the future growth and development of the business – and the staff within it. When you involve more people and staff from all areas are working together, you begin to see those members of your team who can step up, take on more responsibility and make a real difference to the future of the business.

An increase in knowledge

When the business areas share their knowledge and expertise, everything becomes visible. An increase in knowledge helps to attract additional customers through knowing what other departments or business strands can offer them.

Clients and prospects will be impressed by the depth of understanding that you can now bring to them and that will lead them to buy more services from you. The staff at any branch of John Lewis are very knowledgeable about their business and products, and are trained to be able to help customers make the right purchasing decision.

This gives them a competitive edge because they are seen as being expert and customers believe that they are getting good advice and a high standard of service, wherever they are in the country. This makes people want to buy high value items from them because of the perception and reputation that has been built by the company over many years.

Team sharing instead of competing

There will always be an element of competition between departments and business areas within a company, and some healthy competition is good. However, it can also be both destructive and divisive: I have seen businesses performing poorly because they are too focused on the internal politics of the company rather than working for the growth of the business.

One of the ways that this can be stopped – although not overnight – is to get members from different business areas and functions working on projects together. There will already be good teams with high performance and this will make them stronger, creating an edge over the competition and increasing the pool of knowledge about all areas of the company.

The relocation business I worked in did this successfully by having monthly meetings with sales and marketing teams from different areas. These teams had to pool some of their client data and worked towards ways of cross-selling other services into existing customers. In this case it was different relocation services, international, corporate, industrial, business moving and document storage. This seems like an eclectic mix but actually had some good synergies.

It took a while to work, but by having a mandate for change and recognising that there were opportunities to grow the company from the existing customer base, they were able to encourage everyone involved to see that this would make a difference.

Staff met their counterparts in other business areas and learned to share; seeing that this could make a difference to their own performance gave it a value to them as individuals.

Where this could have been further improved would have been to get more of the functions involved – there was no finance representation, for example, and that could have really helped to focus on where to look for the most lucrative opportunities.

The importance of getting personnel to co-operate with each other for the good of the whole business is vital in becoming the best company in a specific sector or market.

More revenue from existing clients

By using a model where different business teams are working together there will be a natural expansion of clients' knowledge about the company and services. Similar to the customer research and profiling, this is about creating the best possible chance of selling additional services to clients who already buy and may not know that they exist.

It can also lead customers to referring the company into their clients' or suppliers' businesses, creating more revenue generating opportunities. But they cannot do this if the business does not give them information. It is up to the company to inform their clients – not the clients to inform themselves. They are already busy operating their own organisations and are unlikely to research what else their suppliers can offer; when you tell them, you are effectively creating another sales channel.

The added benefit is that it costs you less to gain new business from an existing customer than it will to gain a completely new one. The finance department will agree that this is a definite added bonus.

Make sure there is a document, brochure or other communication material that has a section on each of the services, products or business activities that the company offers. This is a simple thing to create, but gives an additional tool to those out selling and looking for opportunities.

It focuses the marketing department on looking at everything and not just their own niche. Going back to the customer research, you will already know what they do not currently buy from the company, enabling each area to create a list of clients for potential cross-selling.

Existing clients in each business area need to be seen as the company's client and not the individual's or the area's client.

Increasing sales at a lower cost to the company is a key factor; pooling client bases and sharing information is a strong way to achieve this and begins to create a different – and much improved – company ethos.

In the office moving part of the relocation company, we acquired a business that was a direct competitor to one of our core business areas. The directive was to keep them separate and competing as they both had established reputations and brands in the marketplace. What actually happened was that they both lost business by focusing on trying to out-manoeuvre each other rather than focusing on the customer.

It would have been far more productive for the business as a whole to have changed the nature of the services that one business provided. The acquired business had a great reputation for logistics – this was quickly lost in the battle for 'top spot'. If the senior management had honed in on the specialist area they could have retained both brands (and reputations), moved any new business leads for non-logistics to the core business and created an influential niche provider.

This would have had a good effect on staff morale – as it was, the acquired company's staff felt like second class citizens – and would have avoided the squabbling and internal politics that ensued.

Internal communication channels

Many companies have an intranet system that enables them to communicate with their staff about what is happening within the business. The intranet is a closed, internal communication channel that can be used to very good effect when harnessed correctly.

However, many of these systems become stale or simply unused because they were created as something that was seen to be necessary rather than something to use proactively.

A good company intranet will be the first port of call for employees to find out what is happening within the company, and should be a priority communication channel. Staff should be targeted with ensuring that there is fresh and relevant content on the intranet each week.

It can also be a place for sharing information and documents between business areas for cross selling – another big advantage in beginning to gain additional revenue from selling services into existing customers.

There could be a spotlight on a certain business area each week, a 'business wins' section, and news or a message from the CEO and senior management. Many companies use this system externally to inform stakeholders or customers about what they are doing and where they are finding success.

The more items of standard company documentation and information that can be made available solely on an internal communications system, the more effectively staff will start to use it. Then, over time, it will become an integral part of the business strategy and communication.

I set up an internal web-based system in the events company I worked in. Internally, the company had several departments that did not operate as a team. It had been allowed to function and develop in this way for so long that it was a part of the culture. We were not going to change that overnight – and probably never completely eradicate it – but by having lots of documentation that each division needed put onto the intranet (and nowhere else), we did encourage staff to begin to use it and start to share best practice.

The addition of news and some mandatory reporting meant that staff began to use and look at it, even when there were a lot of negative comments! It started conversations among staff, which was one of the objectives when it was created.

Updating it could be difficult at times, but it was a battle worth going through as a part of changing the culture to a whole company approach.

Board meetings are often seen within a company as a 'secret' affair. Often happening on a floor of a building or a room where most employees do not visit, there can be an air of elitism about being involved.

The walls need to come down. Not totally, as there are some things that have to be kept behind closed doors or simply are not relevant to everyone, but the intranet is a way of highlighting the key areas that these meetings cover and removing the secrecy and sense of being kept in the dark often felt by employees.

It becomes easier to reach the ideal client, once the profile is written, through sharing and pooling resources within the company. In the same way that business networking groups come together and find the ideal referral for their colleagues, companies can also achieve this.

It may be that the client being sought by one business is already a customer in another area, or a contact of an existing customer or supplier. The people who know this contact may not know that a colleague is looking for them too. Finding a way into them through other areas of the company by sharing knowledge brings down the cost of acquiring them and increases the overall profile of the business.

Consistency, both in approach and materials, also needs consideration. When operating a whole company approach, the marketing materials, branding and messaging must reflect this. Centralise the production of presentations in the same way as using a shared template for the business areas present their review reports; it allows prospective clients to perceive that they are dealing with the same company.

This also aids the brand awareness process that is vitally important to maintain.

Building relationships

Encouraging staff to engage with business areas outside their own roles will increase the awareness of everything the company does, and increase opportunity spotting. When there is a better understanding between departments or teams, there will also be a reduction in friction and an overall increase in productivity.

Instead of the productivity growing in separate areas, it will become more focused towards the objectives of the whole company. Is there potential for part of any company-related bonus scheme to be linked across departments or functions? This will also encourage, albeit in an incentivised way, cross-selling and promotion opportunities.

These relationships will take time to foster, but will result in both better and increased communication.

When I worked for the production and events company, one of my key objectives was to bring together a very disparate group of people who were more used to working against each other – at times it seemed almost for personal pleasure – than they were about growing the business.

This was not restricted to the teams, but also ran through some of the senior management and a board director. The task was virtually impossible to achieve so I had to find small wins that would lead them on very slowly towards a better relationship and working practice.

I started by pairing up members of the sales team with project managers. This meant that at least we had the start of a more effective relationship between the two departments.

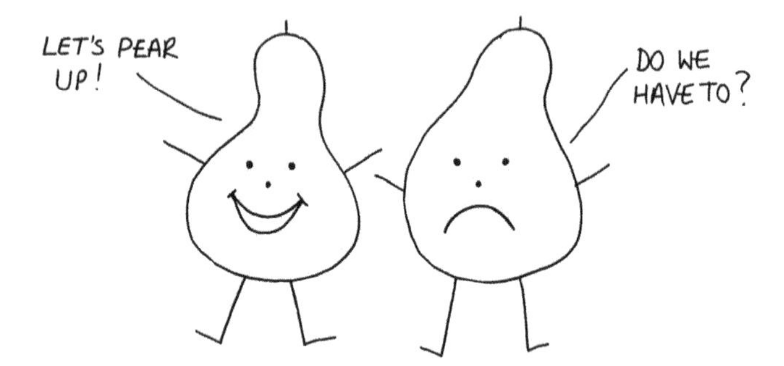

The next thing I did was to merge the customer and prospect sales databases, creating one database that all teams could update with information. They were trained on how to use it together, another part of the 'bonding' process.

Finally, I introduced the company intranet and made sure it was updated every week with news from around the business. I also had a 'library' section created to house policy documents and other materials for use in tender responses, so it became a source for information that people needed to use, and therefore they began to read other areas as well.

None of these things were quick to implement, and they did not solve the whole problem either. What they did do was create an improvement in the situation, a steady increase in co-operation and give the board a good internal communication tool.

It did also mean that the staff paired up together had at least an understanding of what their counterparts did, even if the appreciation was missing! Additionally, it allowed us to see all our customers and prospects in one place, which started the customer profiling process.

Talent will emerge

Choosing staff

There are always talented individuals in companies, but often they do not emerge or are not encouraged to fulfil their potential. If you see and interact with the same people each day, there is rarely the opportunity to find the staff who will make a big impact in the company if given the right direction.

By getting all of the areas and functions of the business working together, talented individuals will begin to emerge. When there is an opportunity for someone to take on a project or work on an acquisition, the default option should not automatically be the head of the business area or department.

A good appraisal system will also find those people in the team who have the ability to step up and take on a new challenge. Appraisals should include talking to staff about where they see – or want – their career to go within the company, but not just filed away for the year when they leave the meeting. HR personnel need to look at these appraisals with the management team.

Time should be spent on highlighted individuals, identifying those who have skills and expertise that could be used to the advantage of the business and the development of the individual.

Asking for volunteers to work on projects to look at developing products or services is another way of finding talent. People who volunteer are keen to demonstrate their worth and step out from under the radar. This can lead to new managers, leadership skills and a good competitive environment for individuals who can make a difference to the company in the future.

Who to watch

Senior management teams will notice who their most productive workers are. Every single one of these will not be the talented individuals – but there will be some among them, those who are striving to get things done over and above their remit, or have a strong work ethic.

Smart CEOs and Finance Directors will have a walk round their company at different times of the day. Talking to people they would not normally see can give a good indication of someone who is ready to move forward. A CEO I worked with was very good at this, and found the talent much more quickly than if he had simply stayed in his office and relied on his teams to alert him to them.

Some staff will also take the initiative of building relationships and links on their own. These people are the future of the company and need to be nurtured, not ignored. You can always fill a gap left by a talented individual whom you have moved, but if you neglect the talent, you will have two gaps to fill when they leave the company to get their next challenge.

A good example of this is a very large tender that the relocation company I worked for wanted to win. It was high profile and only came up for renewal every few years. The workload to create the tender document was huge, and required several staff to come away from what they were doing and focus solely on this project.

This was not in my part of the business, but the team working on the tender sat in a room near me. What was apparent very quickly was that the two key individuals had been selected for their talent, they had not worked together before and both had very different skill sets. The selection was a very good one: they worked well together and emerged having learned new skills and, crucially, winning the contract.

Although both went back to their previous roles, they were called on for advice and to lead teams where large contracts were being bid for. It increased the talent in the business and the opportunity for them to showcase their worth.

Another way of using the talent once you have identified it is to create a business programme within the company. If you do not have a specific role in mind for these individuals, giving them experience of each different department and function within the business is a really good way of finding out where their strengths are and can allow you to place them in the right role when there is an opportunity to do so.

A well-rounded, talented individual will cost the business less to move up than to replace. I had a really talented Marketing Executive in a business I worked in. She needed a challenge. She worked in another part of the business before coming to work with me, and was restricted to the tasks that her role demanded.

I could see that she needed, and was ready, to take on more, so I gave her a whole product to manage. She took on the role in addition to the other duties she had at the time, and flourished. It was an amazing feeling to know that someone else was benefitting from being given an opportunity, and the links with that business area also improved dramatically. She is now the Head of Marketing at a large London company – and they are lucky to have her.

Whilst the company needs talent, it also needs people who are working hard for the growth of the business and not just for their self-promotion. Dominant egos, whilst having a lot of skill, can also be hugely disruptive to the company as their sense of their own stature becomes too large and affects the team dynamic and morale around them.

There are so many things to consider when looking at the talent of the future, but it is vital to the company and can be found much more easily when departments and functions are working together than when everyone is in isolation in their own business area.

Spotting opportunities within the business

Drill into clients

The existing client base within a company can, and should, provide opportunities for additional sales. It is a well known and researched fact that it is less costly to gain additional business from an existing client than it is to acquire a new one.

If a company is not focusing on their existing client base, they will be missing revenue and growth potential. Once a company has created their customer profile, understands their client base well and has staff from all departments and functions working together, the likelihood of finding and capitalising on increased sales from an existing customer will be higher.

Looking closely at the existing customer base is the start of this process.

What do you really know about each of these key customers? Identify who they are, what their business does, and which markets they serve. If you are working with them in one geographical location, they may have other locations where you can add the same value. Similarly, they may have different services or business areas that you do not know exist.

A key task of the marketing department, working with the business area, should be to take each client and research their business. An opportunity may not come from every client, but by being meticulous, nothing will be missed.

Often, business performance targets mean that driving forward to gain new customers is the area of focus. That is why it is important to have the marketing team, in combination with the business development team, looking closely at the current customer base as part of their remit.

Sending the marketing person or team to talk to current customers about what they do and, if possible, what their growth plans are, is a good 'soft sell' way to gain information. Sending a sales or business development person in can be a turn-off to clients because they are always waiting for the sell. A good marketing person will be able to gain more information that will then help when it comes to a sales situation.

I have often been to see clients as part of various roles. Gathering information, not only about them, but also about the level of service we were providing gave good feedback that was used to improve the businesses. I was able to find out different things about them and their market by going to see them as a 'neutral' person. We gained additional sales opportunities as a result of these meetings and were able to solve situations that we did not know existed.

History is also a powerful tool. The current client base was once a prospective client base. Looking back at the very first sale that was made to each client and how they have moved as a customer through the company over time is a key way of determining the future.

When a new sale is made, does the customer gain other quotes, or are they just using you each time? Make sure competitive pricing remains and that complacency does not creep in. I have seen some of my clients using the same suppliers for years: they have a strong relationship with them and see no need to change. Often though, they have not carried out any benchmarking activities to ensure that they are still getting an attractive deal. The supplier may have seen that they are not questioning the prices as they would have done at the beginning of the relationship, so they just keep increasing them over time.

I make sure that my clients are looking at quotes from different companies on a regular basis to ensure that they are receiving value for money and not being used as a cash cow by the supplier. This also enables them to go back and have an informed conversation with their suppliers about the pricing they receive.

In some cases, the suppliers' pricing affects the customers' own client base, so maintaining current information is very important.

Understanding where customers came from originally is another key factor in finding additional revenue opportunities. If they moved from another supplier, what was the reason? Having this information ensures that relationships can be maintained and they continue to be provided with the services that made them a client in the first place.

If the client moved for service level reasons, demonstrating a commitment to continually improving the levels of service to them will result in less reason to go to someone else. If price was the driving force, it is very important to ensure that regular market checks are carried out on the pricing structure used in the company.

Usually it is a combination of both factors. In the previous example, the large contract gained with a government organisation was based on both service delivery and price. The team putting the tender together had to continually research our competitor pricing and also work with the delivery team to ensure that the service standards expected were both being met and exceeded.

Many companies have customers on fixed terms. They need to know well in advance when those contracts are coming near to renewal in order that they can ensure they have the best possible chance of retaining them. Competitors will also be aware of those renewals and will be putting effort into gaining new clients where the service and price expectations are not being met.

Of course, every client cannot be retained, but the key clients and clients identified as potential key clients need to be acted upon. This is not an easy thing to achieve, especially in a larger business, but working towards it will make a difference to the performance of the company in the future.

Ensuring that the right people in the business are talking to the customers is essential. Making sure that relationships are being built at every level that you deal with them at will improve the likelihood of retaining the customer.

Create opportunities for some non-sales contact, for example introduce the CEOs to each other or ask for a tour of their facility. These initiatives demonstrate to the customer that the company is interested and wants to keep doing business with them.

Finding industry news that will be useful to a client is a good reason to contact them. Do not restrict the contact with key customers to just the scheduled review meetings. Good relationships are more likely to be formed outside these meetings, where the key objective is not to talk about sales but to gather and share information.

It is likely that some clients will be good to introduce to each other as well. This will develop their businesses and give your company further credibility. If there is an opportunity to do this, or an obvious synergy between clients, the company should take advantage of it: if all of the customers are kept close and the company does not embrace the benefits that connecting them will bring, there is a significant opportunity lost.

Create niches

One of the most powerful tools that a company can use is to be a specialist, not a generalist. A demonstrable track record of working with clients in a particular market or industry can be used to create a niche.

A niche allows a company to focus on, and become an authority in, one area. It does not mean that you have to say goodbye to all your other clients or stop looking for work in other market sectors, but becoming an authority in one area will bring large benefits in growth and revenue.

It demonstrates expertise and knowledge and assists the company in being known for these qualities within a certain sector. In turn, this means that clients will look for the company and that additional opportunities will be gained – maybe speaking, interviews or articles based on your specific niche knowledge.

The company will be able to present a tighter pitch when targeting new business, one that is clearly focused on what the benefits of using the products and/or services are, concise and deliverable to any audience.

Look at the backgrounds of your staff: where have they worked before and what is their expertise? It may be that they have particular market or industry knowledge that can be used to gain credibility in a certain industry, or have a skill set that lends them to being well placed to move the company into a niche area.

Tap into their experience and use it to leverage the company's strategy and offering.

When the overall company business plan was reviewed, a breakdown of the services and products offered and the marketplaces operated in will have been undertaken. This information can be used to look in detail at where the business has the most profitable work.

Could this information now be applied to specific markets or industries? The company can look at putting together an offering to specific areas or clients which will create a niche.

Again, by looking at the business plan, reviewing, knowing the customers you serve and using staff from different areas of the company, you will be able to identify products and services that are not currently offered, but complement those already offered.

These may be ancillary services, those that will add value to the current offering, and joint ventures or partnerships with other companies. Joint ventures could be relevant with the existing client base, or help to focus on acquiring a client that would be a target for this approach.

Suppliers may provide the platform for a great partnership or joint venture – or they may have a distribution network in place that will enable the company's products and services to reach more clients, and faster.

One of my clients works in performance coaching, providing this service to many different people from a wide range of industries. Recently, she has looked at her business and the current marketplace and has spotted a gap that she can leverage and create a niche in. This 'gap' will focus the business on providing the service range to women, a group that have been identified through analysis of the current customer base and market trends. It is also a group that the business owner feels passionate about.

By recognising this, she has been able to focus her marketing effort into gaining more clients in this sector as she has a demonstrable track record to evidence her experience and industry knowledge.

The growth programme is still in its infancy but is already working. She still has, and is gaining more, customers outside her niche, but now she is beginning to be known for her services and skills in a particular sector of the market.

That niche sector is growing, so she can build a really solid foundation in specifically serving those customers. A great example of creating a niche yet still appealing to the mass market as well.

Combining services

You can also find opportunities through combining existing services to create new offerings that will appeal to both current and new clients. You may have found through the emergence of talent that there are staff with specialist or specific knowledge in an area that will facilitate this.

In the document management business, we operated a specific IT package to manage all of our customers' files internally. This system was also implemented at certain large clients' premises so that they could do the same for their own files.

We had two or three members of staff who knew this system inside out. They were very valuable members of the team and actually helped the software company to iron out issues they had with programming. When we identified the value of these personnel through a business review, we realised that we could sell this expertise to other clients too.

The IT package would then add additional value to the client, and they had the comfort of knowing that we had very experienced personnel to guide and help them. It became an additional service that we could offer in combination with the storage of documents, giving us an additional revenue stream and a competitive edge.

This is an example of how staff working in your business, but maybe in a function rather than the business itself, can add tremendous value to your offering through identifying services that can be sold in combination.

Functional staff can get overlooked in a company. They may have to be there for compliance reasons like health and safety, marketing or finance, but they can hold the key to combining things that are already in place internally to add additional value and sales.

As part of the business review, the company should look at the functional departments and evaluate whether they could be a part of adding additional revenue opportunities.

One of my clients is an independent insurance broker. Highly industry experienced and extremely highly service driven. Their customers do not realise the value of the service they receive, and the work that goes on behind every policy for which they provide a quotation.

This client has been giving insurance advice to her customers for many years, and is now looking at additional revenue streams to grow her business. One of the areas that she is now looking at is charging a fee for the advice she is giving.

The expertise and knowledge that she has is being given away to clients at no cost. Finding a way of packaging this and offering to clients is the next step forward. There needs to be a value placed on what she is currently giving away for nothing.

That is a good example of how revenue and sales opportunities can be extended through existing clients, by looking at the functional departments of your business, and it also goes back to placing a value and worth on what you are selling.

Looking at the marketplace of your customers will also create ideas about what can be packaged together to find additional opportunities. Again, the customer research carried out will be a valuable assistant in this process.

If the customers are happy with the services they are buying and the level of customer service they receive, they are likely to be receptive to new or additional offers, particularly if it will save them time and money on research because they already trust the company.

If you can find ways to combine services and products, have meetings with the clients that you want to target with them. Make specific offerings tailored to clients or markets – or different departments – and visit them to present your thoughts. This will provide information and insight into whether the combinations made are of interest to them, which then allows you to hone the offering.

Segmentation

Make sure that staff have relationships with a customer at more than one level. This will tie in the account and increase the likelihood of retention. If multi-layered relationships are not built and fostered, and your key contact leaves the company, proving your worth with the new incumbent, who will have their own suppliers and relationships coming in with them, is less likely.

There will always be a route into a customer somewhere if the relationships have been built by several different layers of personnel in the business.

What this also demonstrates is that you care about the client. They will see that the company has made the effort to get to know counterparts at every level and so hold a good understanding of their business.

The process of segmentation can begin to happen when the customer database is reviewed and the company really gets to know what makes customers buy. If there are different divisions of a customer company buying, ask for contacts in other divisions that could also want to buy.

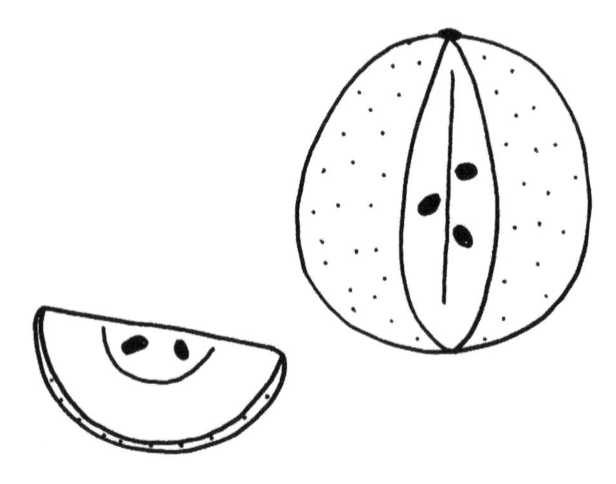

Opportunities to present to several other divisions will be of great benefit and useful in finding additional revenue streams from existing products and services. This will also be a great accolade to the customer who enabled you to sit down with other people in their business.

Interrogation of the customer base leads to highly effective targeting, meaning that time will not be wasted on non-buyers and that the time you spend on real prospects can be increased.

A company I worked for had several high profile clients that they sold to all year round. Occasionally, there would be an opportunity to have a review meeting with them. Over the course of a year or two, we identified that several of these key clients were spending money with our competitors, unaware that we could offer the same service.

We created an in-house 'cell', specifically to provide these services to clients, and focusing on nothing else. It was packaging the services we already offered in a high-end, dedicated version that was appealing. After a lot of work we managed to gain ground and begin to provide a turnkey service on some client projects.

This would not have happened if we had not looked closely at our customer base and identified areas for improvement and advancement.

Segmentation can occur by looking simply at geography. Can the products and services be provided in other locations in the same country – or other countries?

Clients may have overseas facilities and not be using you to deliver their services. Again, the business plan review will tell you whether setting up in a client location would be an additional opportunity for the company.

There can also be 'intangible' services, such as tender writing, advice or added value 'end' services that clients may not be aware of, or that can be set up when you have identified the need for them.

If there are staff who have expertise in writing tender responses and clients who want to win business through a tender process, this also becomes an area with potential for opportunities.

We had a department in the USA that had been created to provide one set of added value services to customers. The operation had been through a teething process and was working well: a gold label support service for the main business.

I went to look at what they were providing and how we could use the geographical time difference to provide the same services on a 24-hour basis in the UK, giving their customers the ability to have 24-hour service provision due to the time zone differential.

The business model was sound and relatively simple to replicate – another example of how different parts of the company can be harnessed to work together and provide increased sales and revenue wherever in the world they happen to be.

By using all of these tactics, the company will be able to find the opportunities that already exist in the business areas, with customers that they already have. In combination with reviewing the whole business plan, building a customer profile and knowing the customers needs, 'wants' can be anticipated and additional revenue growth created from them.

Summary

- Involving everyone increases sales opportunities
- Include all services and products (or a summary of them) in communication materials
- Review company documentation to ensure consistency
- Search for talent that exists in the business – and use it!
- Look for niche areas to increase specialism

5

Make your marketing work harder

There are many ways that marketing can be used successfully to increase growth in a company. This chapter focuses on strategies and tactics to get good marketing practice embedded throughout the business.

Look at the structure of your team

Many businesses are not marketing led. By harnessing the marketing team in the right way, a company can make big strides forward with growth. If the marketing team just exists to create communications materials and follow a plan that has been in place for many years, full benefit will not be gained from them.

Marketing personnel have skills and expertise that should be used as much as possible. To make sure that you are achieving the maximum return from your marketing look first at the existing structure, roles and personnel in the team.

In some companies, the marketing department consists of one person, and there are many businesses where the marketing role is shared with another functional role and the job time split between the two.

If that is the case, are they a marketing specialist or are their skills in the other portion of their job, and marketing just landed with them? This is not ideal for a key functional area that should be helping to drive the business forward.

Sometimes I work with clients who do not have a marketing function at all. Sometimes this is because they are too small to carry the overhead at first, and others just have not really seen the need to employ someone in this role.

What they are missing out on by not having the skills that a good marketer can bring them is the ability to grow and develop at a faster and more effective rate than they are seeing at present.

When you look at your marketing structure, is it right? Given the review of the business plan, customer understanding and cross-function working, could the roles be more effective if the structure was changed?

If the marketing team are working in a head office location, they need to go and work at the coal face of the business for a time to gain a real understanding of what the company provides to customers and how the products and services are delivered. This will end any ivory tower syndrome that may be happening, and also show the business areas that they are a real part of the company's overall growth and change.

As the company grows, you might need additional staff or different expertise to move forward. With the emergence and growth of social media (for example), there are skills that might not already be in the company but are necessary to keep up with and embrace these new areas of marketing.

Have the staff had any formal training; are they reading relevant marketing publications each week and keeping up to date with the methods that are being employed in the wider business world? Ideas can be generated by reading about what someone else is doing, and they could come from a completely different marketplace.

Training is not only confined to increasing their skill set in marketing areas. Send the marketing team onto the same internal training that operational or customer service, or other staff are attending. This will give them further insight into the whole company activity and improve their knowledge and understanding.

Cross training will also make them more visible in the business, increasing their credibility and stopping them from being seen as detached or remote from the daily operation activity of the company.

I worked my way from answering a telephone helpline and sending out magazines, to working in an operational branch for a couple of years before winning a junior marketing job. From there, over a period of time, I became the Marketing Manager for five business-to-business areas.

Today this is unusual – it may have been then too – but what it gave me was an extensive knowledge of the company I worked for from the ground up. This then helped enormously when marketing the services that we provided to our clients.

I had many connections with people who worked in the service delivery areas and could gain feedback and insight far more quickly than some of my colleagues who had only ever been in the marketing department at head office.

It would have been very useful for everyone in the various marketing departments to have spent time with the operational branches – they would have been more accepted and been able to judge how effective their marketing ideas would be, and where improvements and support were needed.

I make it a point now, with any new client, to be as nosey as possible about all areas of their business – not just the one they have asked me to look at. I have found lots of opportunities and simple changes that have increased growth and added additional revenue, just by asking lots of questions about the whole business.

As the market changes and industries move in different directions, with the internet playing an ever-increasing role, a regular review of department structure and roles is crucial. A need for additional staff might be identified – a specific skill area where there is a gap (or less understanding than is needed) – and this should be monitored closely as it will, and should, have an impact on the whole company.

Sometimes difficult decisions are necessary if, for example, you identify staff who need to be replaced. Although these decisions are hard to make, they must be taken quickly so that the company has the right skills and expertise to deliver the growth and performance required.

I have seen staff who needed to be moved or replaced and yet were left in their roles because the management team were reluctant to take action. In every single case this had a detrimental effect on the business, and in one case it actually led to a spiral that could not be easily reversed and damaged the performance of the overall business significantly.

Succession planning is also a key part of reviewing the team structure. If there is only one marketing person in the company, make sure you understand what the effect would be if and when they leave the company. Is there someone who can be identified as an emerging talent and could begin to work alongside that person to accumulate knowledge and provide additional skill?

Introducing a non-exec director who has a marketing background will also increase the knowledge and experience base of the company – particularly where marketing is a one-person role. This will strengthen the overall marketing function; they can add huge value to the business and be an objective voice as they are not involved in the daily operation of the company.

If there is a team of marketing personnel, look at where they can work together to gain an understanding of each other's roles to aid the succession planning process. This could be on a cross-product project or, more simply, by having a regular joint meeting to discuss what they are working on in their area of the business. These meetings can also foster a team ethic and throw up ideas that can be used elsewhere in the company, or in other business areas.

A marketing team that has been in place for a long time and not updated skills training or immersion into the operational areas of the business, or into other functions such as finance, will not be supporting the growth of the company effectively.

Companies need to make sure that their marketing teams are constantly acquiring new skills and knowledge to enable them to improve their performance in the company, have new ideas and test them, and importantly, challenge the business over their existing marketing approach.

The marketing team need to be involved with customers, too. They should be meeting customers and be a part of any pitching or presentations to prospective customers. They are the eyes and ears of the business and, if left in a separate area, cannot share the value and advice that they have, making them a wasted resource.

In the relocation company, I worked in the business services department, and there were two other Marketing Managers working in domestic, international and corporate relocation areas. We all had an extensive knowledge of our products and services, either through working in different areas of the business, and partly as a result of having been with the company for a long time.

Being attached to a business area meant that we were involved in the whole business and not just confined to the marketing department. This took a long time to achieve but it was beneficial to each of the businesses and the company as a whole.

Although we all sat together, we were each focused on our own area with no cross-over or sharing of information. Until we started to break down the barriers between us we were not as effective for the whole company as we could have been.

The CEO decided to change the structure of the marketing function radically. Instead of having marketing within the business, they chose to physically relocate the whole marketing function to a different place and create completely different roles.

As a consequence of this they lost two of us, and in fact the whole team from my business area. A lifetime of knowledge disappeared from the company in a matter of months, with no one gathering even a small percentage of the experience that we had.

This is an example of a major change in the way that marketing was structured. The company felt that it was right for the business, although the business areas did not feel that it was the right thing for them at the time.

If you look at the structure of the department and decide to make changes that are fundamental, make sure the options have been reviewed and that plans are in place for all of the possible outcomes that may occur: staff may leave, continuity may be affected for a time and morale needs to be kept high. If knowledge is leaving the business, how will the new team gain this knowledge? It may not be important for them to be as immersed in the business, but the company will benefit far more if they are.

Is the budget in the right place?

The marketing budget can be a contentious issue! Where to allocate it: if there are different business areas, should one have the lion's share or should it be spread equally? Is it a decision based on the previous year and the year before that, with simply a percentage rise and the same items being produced or activity being carried out?

I have often seen marketing budgets allocated based on the budget given the previous year, with a small increase. This is not the ideal way to allocate the budget for the year.

If the business plan has been reviewed, the profiling carried out and the customer research made, the marketing budget allocation should be a reflection of what is needed for the company, not what has been given historically.

If growth is required in certain services, or one business area is growing quickly, the right amount of funding needs to be allocated to those areas to ensure the performance is maintained or increased again. When there is an opportunity to really make a difference to the business, it needs to be taken and history put to one side.

In the relocation business, the budget was allocated in a largely historic way. The core service gained the largest share and then the other services gained a lesser share. This often meant that we were only able to stand still instead of really moving our business areas forward, because we simply did not have the capital to do anything else.

I simply accepted my portion without making a good enough case for why we should have more. If I had tried harder, I might not have succeeded, but at least our business areas would have been noticed for wanting to improve performance through additional investment.

Now I look at businesses spend areas and make recommendations based on what their needs are now and not what their rationale may have been two or three years ago – or even last month. It often helps to have an objective opinion from someone outside the company, too, acting as a sense check. It can really help to confirm the decisions being made are right for the business.

Begin with what is being spent now, and assess what impact it would have if you spent that budget on different activities than those currently used. Could you improve the rate of return by moving part of the budget into an alternative activity?

Often, a marketing budget is put together on the strength of the activity undertaken in the previous year, or two years or three years. This is the classic 'what we have always done' approach, with one or two new elements dropped if the budget is not increased by the percentage rate that is usually given.

Consider taking the marketing plan in line with the business review and all the other extensive research that is now being carried out. Knowing more about your existing customers and having created the profile for the customer of the future, you can now take a clear view on where your marketing activity needs to be.

One of the exercises I carry out with my clients is to make a list of all of the areas where they spend on marketing, and the amounts they spend next to them. We then look at the return they gain from each of these activities (recognising that some cannot be measured – or that a judgement has to be made), and from that we can get a rough idea of where the current budget is having an impact.

Then we look at other areas of activity not currently used and evaluate whether they would be more beneficial than those on the list. In this way we are sense-checking the budget and making sure that the client's spend is delivering them value.

In addition to looking at the spend on marketing, broken down by business area, take into account, as well, what the money is actually spent on. Sometimes you will find that a business area has taken some of the marketing budget to fund non-marketing related areas. Whilst there may be movement of budget in a business area, moving it away from the vehicle that drives customers to your door is not usually the most sensible solution.

When looking at what the money is spent on, making a list of activity, cost and the percentage amount it represents overall gives a clear picture of the current situation.

There may be some items in the budget that are 'must haves'. These can often include maintaining the website, communication materials, PR and online marketing services such as SEO. They are constant business needs, but even so, they may warrant fresh evaluation. Do the communication materials still meet the needs of the prospective customer – especially given that a comprehensive profile has been compiled? Can they be produced in a different size or even as an electronic document? It may be that the materials can be produced in smaller quantities or that they need to change in terms of design or finish. If they do not meet the needs of the client profile they should be re-evaluated.

It is as important to address the fundamental 'must haves' as to evaluate the new activities. Just because the business needs something, it may now be possible (or necessary) to change the way it is produced or how it looks. These items should not just be put to one side and the focus moved on to the new additions; they are equally, if not more, important.

Checking these areas may actually reveal the need for additional budget to make changes or create new items. The materials used to communicate the key company messages to clients are vitally important, they have to reflect the type and quality of product and service that is being offered. This includes the 'must have' items and is not restricted to printed materials.

Another question to consider is whether the areas of spend reflect the performance and growth of the business. If they are historic activities, are they still delivering the return the company needs? If the business area is performing strongly and has an aggressive growth target, the marketing budget should reflect this.

Making an investment in a growth area should not be restricted to an additional member on the sales team or the purchase of new equipment – the message needs to get to the prospective customers to encourage them towards the sales team. This is driven by the marketing activity.

Some of the budget should be allocated to retaining existing customers, whether that is on an event, meeting, trip or additional communication. Retention is vitally important; it is less costly to keep an existing customer than to acquire a new one, and this can be an area that is overlooked when budgets are put together.

The retention budget does not need to be large, but enough to make a positive impact on the customer. There may be things specific to your industry or market that are appropriate to allocate spend to, or you may just want to mark Christmas or an anniversary milestone with them each year.

Following on from the customer needs research, it is also possible that having a meeting with them or introducing them to other clients is what needs to be done.

Next, review the marketing spend against the customer profile you have created. This will enable the company to check that the spend reflects and matches the type of customers that are desired.

Knowing where improvements can be made will have a direct impact on the effectiveness of the marketing activity. If you have been carrying out mass marketing, now is the time to look at strategic, targeted marketing that reaches the right prospective clients and leaves out those who will never buy.

Some mass marketing activity may remain to maintain brand awareness, but when the niche area has been established and the customer profile defined, strategic activity can be put into place.

Ask customers what they read. Are there certain publications that they will look at and others that might find their way straight into the bin? This will provide information that can be used as part of the research into where the advertising budget is best allocated, and the type of activity that will appeal to the target customers.

At the relocation company, we used to advertise in our own industry publications and did not have a huge budget to spend. By talking to our customer groups we found that they read specific publications that we had never looked at advertising in before. This enabled us to change our approach and have an 'industry' or niche voice within several of our client groups by taking space and writing an 'advice column' advert each month that was relevant to their specific market.

Our results in terms of new clients were improved; we would not have secured new business by simply having an advert in our own industry magazine. We needed to go out to the niches we had chosen and build up expertise in language, style and content that would appeal to them.

Whilst advertising is difficult to directly measure in terms of a straight lead generation return, it is often a necessary part of the company's marketing activity. By honing the customer profile and carrying out customer research you can make sure that your advertising is strategic, targeting key groups of customers, industries and markets.

The bottom line is that when knowledge is increased by carrying out reviews, research and profiling, decisions about marketing spend become clear and directed to the people you want to gain as customers.

Summary

- Review the marketing function – are the correct roles in place?
- Evaluate different budget allocation strategies
- Check that the marketing budget reflects the performance and growth of the business
- Match the marketing programme to your target audience – research and profile
- Make sure that you have some budget for retention activities

6

Reviewing suppliers

Suppliers play an important role in marketing. They can create opportunities for additional sales, and building strong relationships with them brings flexibility and competitive pricing. Along with this, measuring and reviewing marketing activity is also vital. Analysis gives control and enables changes to be made when they are needed. Both these areas form the basis of this chapter.

We all have suppliers who we work with to deliver results to our customers. Having good supplier relationships is very important as it enables the company to gain trusted advice and a confidence that they are delivering exactly what you need, at the right price and time.

Often, supplier pricing will have a direct effect on company pricing, so conducting a regular review process with suppliers is vital.

Look at what you are spending with each supplier and how the prices have changed over the course of a six to 12 month period. When I am delivering services for my clients, I benchmark the prices I get from my regular suppliers to ensure that I am getting competitive quotes and am able to pass these onto customers.

If there is a supplier with whom the company spends a large amount, it is useful to get them to re-tender to you, presenting and pitching their services. Good suppliers will do this as a proactive exercise because they will want to retain you as a customer and will also be looking for ways they might, in turn, be able to increase their revenues.

Are your larger suppliers on a fixed contract? How often are they reviewed and what is their pricing level in comparison to their competitors who are offering the same service?

Spending should not only be reviewed on price. The relationship is important: it has taken time and resource to build, and increasing the supplier's knowledge about the client company is important too. They will be better able to serve you and may be able to save you money or change processes when they know you more.

This is where the supplier's value to your business also comes into consideration. Time spent building relationships and establishing working methods will have to be repeated if a supplier is switched on a purely cost-driven basis.

Just like the customer research, it is important to know exactly what the supplier can offer. Do you know everything that they provide? There may be other areas where they can assist the business that the company is not aware of. They may also have ideas that will help the business, maybe in logistics or in a different service, that will meet a number of your strategic goals and improve performance.

Talk to them about your clients: give them a good opportunity to understand more about what the business areas provide so that they can add value. Ask your suppliers about their customers, too. They may have good contacts for you to be introduced to, or opportunities for partnerships between your clients and theirs.

Equally, your clients may also be able to refer the supplier on. This will also increase your value, visibility and credibility.

Spending time with key suppliers is an important part of the marketing process. It ensures that the best possible customer service and competitive pricing are received, and it enables them to add value to the business by understanding it well and therefore being in a position to make suggestions and present fresh ideas.

Measuring effectively

Measuring marketing activity can be difficult, depending on the areas of spend. Some activities are easily measured and monitored, giving results that enable the business to make changes and amendments to the programme on a regular basis, while others may be harder to quantify.

Exhibitions and advertising can pose measurement issues as they are partly carried out to increase or maintain band awareness (for example), and cannot only be counted or analysed as a pure lead generation exercise.

Having a set of measurement criteria is critical, though, as all marketing activity should be reviewed and assessed on the benefit brought to the company. This may be in the number of sales made against the cost, or the number of enquiries generated surrounding the activity. There may also be perceived benefits to the company such as an increase in the number of visits to a website or to a certain section or page of the website.

Whichever methods are chosen, having a process for measurement means that the activity can be monitored and challenged. If the activity is not meeting the measurement criteria, it needs to be investigated before being dropped or changed.

It may be that there is a reason why this is not working currently: time of year, buying patterns, an unexpected market shift, sometimes even changes in the weather can affect revenues. These reasons might not be the same in two months' time, so the activity could be suspended until the climate is better placed to deliver results.

When challenging the current activity, think about what the consequences would be if you stopped doing it. If the perceived impact on the business would be significant, it might be better to scale back that area of marketing rather than remove it completely while it is being evaluated and analysed.

For example, a very traditional, UK based consumer services company I worked for, used paper directories as 90% of their advertising spend each year. The consequences of an incorrect telephone number appearing on an advert was huge: revenue would be severely affected and in some cases it could cause a branch to close down completely.

Then came the internet. Customer buying patterns and, specifically, information gathering methods changed significantly. The company was very reluctant to make the leap to a different way of attracting clients. This was understandable, given that the directory advertising method had been the cornerstone of sales for decades.

In this case, the approach had to be changed very slowly with testing and measurement processes in place for each new activity. This was repeated until the company was confident about investing in different marketing methods.

The breadth and detail of analysis tools available to measure and monitor online marketing activity has improved greatly and changed beyond imagination from even a couple of years ago. Tracking of the impact that advertising and SEO is making to the traffic being driven to the website is very comprehensive. This enables businesses to make decisions quickly about where their marketing spend would be best used, and where it is having the most effect.

Setting targets for the marketing team based on the measurement and effectiveness of their activity is also a good method to employ. This increases accountability and focuses the team on making sure that they are implementing programmes that produce results; changing one or two activities at a time – not everything at once – is the right approach to take.

The same goes for the business areas and functions. Everyone has a part to play in marketing the company, and having some of their target or performance objectives connected to marketing as well as revenue and profit is a really effective way of bringing marketing and the business together – and placing focus on the importance of marketing.

In the international relocation company I worked for, my bonus criteria were set on meeting certain marketing objectives during the year: creating a website, setting up a database, and so on. Really, I should have had a target that included revenue growth or profit of the business area I was working in. Likewise, the operational team should have had a target that included a marketing element.

In effect, I could have focused solely on my objectives as I did not have any incentive to be aware of what the business was achieving. This is an area that companies need to address, as marketing should be a part of the whole business, making a contribution and seen as central to growth. Equally, marketing teams need to understand the business they are working in and be a part of the overall performance indicator. Using measurement tools in combination with objective setting and regular review is the key to this, and the key to making the marketing budget work hard for the company.

Summary

- Benchmark supplier pricing regularly
- Understand everything that your suppliers can provide
- Present your business to your suppliers
- Measure and monitor your marketing activity
- Set objectives tied to business performance

7

Get advice from outside

It is very easy to become blinkered when you are running a business. Focusing on all the areas that need attention and growing the company means that you can lose objectivity. Bringing in a specialist from outside the company can really help to see things from a different perspective, and this chapter looks at why this is so important.

Specialist feedback

When the business plan was reviewed and the customer profiling carried out, there will have been challenge from the internal teams working on these areas and also from the CEO and senior management. In fact, if the cross-function approach was used, there will have been lots of challenge from many areas within the company.

That is very important because it helps to shape plans in the right way, getting ready to take them out to the marketplace and really test them. Even when objections have been difficult to overcome and full agreement may not have been gained, the fact that the discussions and opinions were voiced makes a positive difference to the outcome of the future plans.

The next stage is also very important and is not always implemented. Once all of the internal conversations and discussions, meetings and reviews have taken place, it is the right time to gain some advice and feedback from outside of the company.

Bringing in someone from outside the business to sense-check and challenge the strategy again is a robust way of ensuring that all the planning and research work that has been carried out is strong, tested and well thought through.

Having an objective specialist looking at what the company has been planning and preparing is not a sign of weakness. It is actually a great show of strength. Companies that do this are in a better position to succeed and drive forward in their markets and industries.

This advice may come from a consultancy company, marketing specialist or business adviser. It needs to be someone who can be completely honest and has no ties to the business. Having no ties to the industry or marketplace that the company operates in is a strong advantage.

Having no long standing links to an industry means that there is no history and also no 'previous' knowledge or experience of activity implemented in a previous role or company. You are gaining unbiased advice from someone who understands how businesses operate and is able to recognise areas that may be improved or changed very quickly.

A good combination of skills to look for in an outside voice are having worked in different areas and levels of business before reaching the peak in their own area of expertise or niche.

If they have worked in many different departments or business areas within companies during their career path, before finding their own specialism, the outsider will be able to view things from a multi-layer perspective and should be able to communicate effectively with all levels in a business.

Check that your objective outsider is established and has a clear and proven track record of working in this field, and that it is their main source of income, before they are engaged. See several different specialists to make sure that the one chosen is right for your business and will have the biggest impact.

Ask for case studies and examples of their work; follow up references with their clients. The company needs to be sure that they will be working with someone who has the experience and personal qualities to derive the maximum benefit possible for the business.

A specialist may have their own processes and questioning sets that they have developed whilst working with clients. They will have a skill in their area of expertise and will be passionate about what they do. This in turn will enable them to gain buy-in from other members of staff and an ability to lead discussions and move conversations forward.

When I was given a special project in the relocation company that involved working in the international and corporate sectors of the business both in the UK and America, I took some time out to think about how I would handle the situation. We had a corporate moving division in the UK, relocating families from companies where a job change meant a new location. A range of 'settling' services was being looked at to help the families adjust to their new town or city quickly and settle in. These would include finding schools for children and ensuring that they knew where to find all the local amenities.

This service already existed in our American corporate moving division, and I had to look at what we could learn from them and whether there were any opportunities to combine the services in both countries.

I was seen as an 'invader' in a business area in which the team believed that someone within their own ranks should have been leading this project. It was not easy to break through those barriers and gain the information that I needed to enable me to give the best advice that I could about the project's viability.

Some of the team in America also gave me a reasonably hostile reception as they too felt that a representative from within their own business area should have been chosen.

I had to draw on all my resources. Having worked in businesses from the ground up, I was used to communicating with people from different areas, job roles and functions and this stood me in good stead. It helped me to manage the situation I was in and enabled me to succeed. I was able to gain a great deal more information from the American team operating the service because I had previously worked in operations and understood the right questions to ask.

These are examples of the skills and attributes a specialist that is brought into the company should have:

An objective voice

Using the services of someone not in the market or industry that the company is in is really critical. If the specialist is not in your company or sector, they can tell it how it is, listen hard and spot things that you will not.

The objective voice has no allegiances within the business. They can be integrated at a level where more of the staff will share information that would otherwise never get to the CEO and senior management team, but could be hugely relevant.

One of my clients has a jewellery business that is very exciting. They were receiving a great deal of advice from nearly everyone they came across at networking events about who they should be targeting, and were given a lot of contacts. The company was aiming for a very high end client base and while the owner had the skill to deliver outstanding products, they were lacking the business skills to both gain meetings with the desired prospects and also to close deals.

As a result of this, a large proportion of their time was spent networking, in the right places, but their personal business and marketing acumen was not sufficient to capitalise on the opportunities. The other result was that the company was spending more and more money on materials to make products that showcased their work, and not being paid for them.

They did not understand their cost base and were often under-pricing by a huge margin for the work that they were gaining. As I had no allegiance to them, and no ties to their business, I was able to give honest advice and feedback to them – not necessarily what they wanted to hear, but suggestions that would make the difference between them surviving and not.

We talked about pricing. This was the first item that they needed to address, and quickly. Once they understood what the costs were to make a product, they could then see what their worth was and the level at which they needed to be pricing.

This immediately meant that they could stop having long conversations with people who were not prepared to pay for the skill, and focus them on targeting the prospects who were. It also gave them confidence because they could now evidence the costs and were able to have conviction that their pricing level was right.

The other piece of advice that I gave them was to scale back the operation in the short term to enable them to start making a profit. Starting a business that wants to sell directly into high value clients or a luxury market from the outset can be achieved, but it needs a number of factors and financial resources that this company simply did not have.

By scaling back the business for a while, they were able to make products for a different market that were affordable and that in turn made them some profitable revenue while they focused on writing a marketing plan to take the company into their target niche market. They are now implementing this and making decisions that are leading to the growth of the business.

A specialist has no historical 'baggage' from outside the business. They can come in without the politics that exist within every company, no matter how big or small, fresh and unencumbered.

If they are like me, they will be nosey! I like to ask lots of questions to really understand the business and how it operates, probing the areas that need to be explored in more detail. A specialist will also listen hard and watch closely what happens as they move through the company. They will be able to alter their communication approach with different people and departments when they need to, empathise and take an alternative line of questioning.

There will always be members of a team or department who are wary of someone coming into their area and asking questions. It can be unsettling, even if they understand and buy into the reasons for having advice and feedback from outside. When looking to work with someone from outside the business, people skills and management are key criteria to look for, as well as ensuring that there is a good cultural fit.

There is no point in spending money on a resource, however good, if they will not be able to work effectively at all levels in the company to achieve the objectives that have been set.

An objective voice will need information and some guidance before commencing their work. They will need to have some brief background information on the members of the team they will be liaising with, a clear set of objectives to achieve, and some guidance on any specific information needed, or specific questions to be asked.

This is the time to reflect on and review the business plan, and all the surrounding customer work carried out to, make sure that the feedback assimilated will meet the objectives.

A key advantage of using an objective voice is that the person coming into the company will be able to ask, and get answers to, the questions that the CEO and senior management team find it hard to obtain. Sometimes this can be information needed from within the senior management team, where there may be conflict or other issues that are preventing the flow of information.

The international events company I worked in had a disparate senior management team. They hid information from each other and in some cases actively made it difficult for other departments to be effective in their areas.

In this case I had to be the objective voice. I did not come to my role with any baggage, I had not worked in the events and production industry before, so I was able to gain information and ask the questions that meant we could begin to overcome some of the barriers and roadblocks that had been established.

This was not done quickly, and indirect methods had to be used to break down the issues that had been created. We looked at key personnel within the departments who had influence and respect from other staff, and then worked with them to gain buy-in and spread a positive message.

This helped to dilute the problems being faced and enabled us to work more effectively for the good of the company. We began by bypassing those who were never going to change their behaviour, and so we were able to make a difference to the business. In the longer term, we had to manage the behaviour of the 'roadblocks' and work on making a shift in their learned working and behaviour patterns.

This did not solve all the issues, but it did mean that we could continue to grow and work to meet key objectives, and over time to meet less hostility.

A different angle

Clear and fresh thinking leads to better planning, and should be used to challenge current plans and thoughts of the company's leadership team.

Someone coming in from outside is not part of the marketing team, board or senior management team of the company. This puts them in the unique position of being able to see the whole business from a different angle, and enables them to have an overview of the company, seeing the big picture.

They are also able to be the eyes and ears of the CEO, getting to the parts of the business and gaining feedback and answers to questions that may not be able to be tackled on an internal, daily, or even yearly, basis.

Is there a better way to do something that is currently being done? Is there a way to work additional revenue from a business area that is not currently utilised to its full potential? Someone with sound business and marketing knowledge can get to the root of these questions and often spot processes, and even products or services, that could be improved and lead to sales and profit generation.

They will challenge the current thinking of the leadership team, making sure that the business plans and marketing programmes in place are robust and right for growth or game-changing.

Using the skill of an objective, experienced individual or consultancy can be carried out in different ways. I have been brought in, and seen others brought in, to tackle a single product or service in a company. They needed additional support and feedback to evaluate the growth potential and challenge the plans. At other times, a complete evaluation of a company's plans and strategy is needed, or a review of the marketing function and activity.

Sometimes, consultants can come in to look at processes or cost reduction in part or all of the company, and sometimes advice might be needed in one specific functional area such as sales, marketing or finance.

A company needs to ensure that an incoming specialist will give them good value. Making sure that objectives are set and agreed to at the beginning, and having timelines and specific outcomes through the process – just as the company would set for performance internally – are imperative.

If value is not being added and the business does not see this until the end of the project, there will be no point in having them there and the process will have to begin again with someone new. This is more likely to be the case where there are no agreed objectives and outcomes, and no regular review.

This can, and does, happen, and often turns a CEO against having outside advisers entering the company again. Unfortunately, this can then stop or slow down company growth because it is an important part of the marketing process as a whole. Making sure that the milestones are in place at the beginning, clearly and agreed to by both parties, is key.

Things do go wrong sometimes, through personality or the wrong type of help being sought, but if the rules are in place from the start, the process can be stopped quickly if it is not achieving the right result.

By drawing on their experience, a good objective adviser will know what will work, what has a good chance of working, and how to achieve success. A different angle should also provide a competitive edge with no internal roadblocks. Being able to question, advise and generate feedback often gives insight into talented individuals who have not been spotted and into areas where changing personnel, or introducing a new role, might make a very big difference.

Selecting the right help

The first item needed, when looking to engage the help and advice from an external source of any kind, is a plan.

In the same way as going through the overall business strategy, reviewing the strategy and then building the customer profile and the marketing effort, a clearly defined plan is vital to the successful outcome.

What does this person or organisation need to deliver; what do you want and need them to do? Should they have a business background or just a marketing background? My suggestion would be both. The maximum value will be gained from having a consultant or team in the company who have worked at many levels and functions within a business as their careers have progressed – and not just in a marketing role.

It is my belief that this is important for a number of reasons.

Primarily, when someone has held job roles in many areas of business, they will have gained a lot of different skills and been exposed to many different processes, operations and people.

This naturally makes them able to work and communicate with staff, whatever their level or position in a company. Why is this important? Key insights can come from someone outside the leadership or senior management team. Someone who has no voice, who does not want to be 'at the top', and who seldom gets heard will be in a position to give powerful feedback.

Unlocking these points of view, discarding those that are not important or credible, and then looking at how to use those that are, is really invaluable. Someone who has worked everywhere will be able to do this. A person who has high levels of skill in one area or discipline where they have worked their entire career, maybe marketing or finance, operations or sales, will not have this breadth of experience, and that is really what a company employing an objective voice should be looking for.

If a person with expertise in one area comes into a company as a specialist, they will give value in the one area where their skills lie. That in itself is not a negative thing, but it will only address issues that are in their comfort zone, and not highlight those outside that discipline.

When I worked at the relocation company as a Marketing Manager, the industrial moving division had a consultant brought in by the CEO. The consultant was a marketer, a very good one. The issue with this business area was that they were not marketing led – it was taking me a long time, with lots of barriers to break down, to become part of the team; a 'marketing consultant' was not going to get to the issues that surrounded the business, in their view.

Barriers were put up and although they were given all the information they requested, they got no further help or insight from the team, who complied with what they were asked for and nothing more. The resulting report and analysis was virtually worthless. This was not the fault of the marketing consultant, but a failure on the part of the CEO to recognise that someone with ground-up business experience was needed to really get to the heart of things and add value.

Someone who has a good knowledge of how a business works will also see the missing links. If they have a background purely in one area, they will be less likely to see how other functions and departments fit within the company. An individual who has been involved in many different areas has the opportunity to deliver much more value because they will be able to connect everything and understand more easily how the aspects operate together.

I have worked with many clients in a wide variety of industries. Many of their target markets are not markets that I have worked in before. The principles of the work I do remain the same whatever the market, and the issues they are facing are varied so I can draw on all my experience to make sure that they receive the best possible advice and feedback.

They gain from the fact that I have worked in many different roles across lots of industries. Being tied to one industry or market, or having only worked in a marketing department, would not assist me in my role now, and would not benefit my clients.

I have spotted issues and solved sales problems for my clients, without having been experienced in their business, because I know what to look for as a result of having spent time in operations, sales, marketing, and so on.

So the broad expertise of the person coming in is more relevant, and far more important, than having a good knowledge of your specific industry.

The specialist feedback being sought, whether on the whole business plan, a specific service or product, or a specific function, should be coming from an expert – not from a friend, as also quite often happens. A friend of a CEO or Senior Management team may have set up in business on their own, providing the type of consultancy or business advice that the company is now looking for.

In my opinion, hiring that person is rarely a good idea. The feedback gained needs to be objective, and a friend cannot be totally objective, even if the person introducing them has no part in the process. There will always be an association present, making information gathering and answers to difficult questions far less possible.

If it is really felt that this person would be the perfect objective voice, they should be selected out of a number of other candidates, all of whom should meet the senior management team to enable a comparison and sense-check to take place. This will also provide a benchmarking opportunity on the price, objectives and methods they propose.

Although cost is another area that will always be a consideration, in my opinion this should not be a key factor of the decision making process. The most important thing is that they are the right person to be working with the company to deliver the maximum possible value.

If they are expensive, then in the medium to long term it would be worth asking them to take a non-exec directorship. This will retain the expertise and challenge for the company, and provide reward for the value that has been added. It is worth thinking about a longer-term relationship with someone who is providing specialist advice, as they will be able to assist with growth and areas of issue in the future, or assist with role transition or structural changes.

Finding the right person or organisation has to follow a process. The first stage is to plan for the work that needs carrying out, the objectives and targets, and the type of person who would be right for the project.

The 'finding' part should not just be left to a recruitment specialist, but should also be researched. Have any other companies or contacts used someone who they felt added real value? A recommendation is always a good place to start, as long as they can demonstrate a good track record and are not just the friend of a fellow CEO!

Check their credentials with their clients. Ask to speak to at least two clients on the telephone, in just the same way as references are taken up for a salaried role.

Make sure that your criteria are met. If there are many criteria, this may not always be easy, or entirely possible, but the most important criteria must be fulfilled. Have a list of the qualities and attributes that are needed in this person, both personally and in their skill set – in the same way as building the customer profile gives both the demographic and psychological elements that were needed to create the ideal target.

Once the plan is in place you will be able to go out to the market and find the right person or organisation to work with. This can be as a combination of recommendations and candidates sourced by trusted people, using the criteria and person specification that has been set.

Selecting the right person is critical: it should be viewed in the same way that recruiting a senior role in the company would be, in order to gain the most value and achieve results.

Summary

- An outside voice should sense check and challenge
- Find the right skill set for *your* company
- Set the objectives and meet regularly
- Open up communications at all staff levels
- Recruit as if you were employing a senior executive

8

Trying something new – the game-changer

Finding a game-changer or trying something new in a company is a big undertaking. However, it is something that can transform the nature and size of the company, taking it to a different level, new markets, additional industries and increased geographical locations.

The idea

The place to begin work on trying something different is looking within the existing business. In some ways, this is similar to looking for additional opportunities, but instead of these opportunities coming from bases already in the company, they are the springboards to jumping outside.

Look at the markets that the company operates in. Research the key markets, where they are now, how they are forecast to change and what the influences are on them. Information about all of these factors can be gathered from senior personnel, identified companies, independent bodies and umbrella organisations.

Independent research could also be commissioned, either as a bespoke piece or as part of an omnibus piece where several companies take part (in this case, they are able to ask some specific questions in addition to the fixed questions that the survey will cover).

An obvious area for looking a game-changer is geography. There are many emerging economies and markets that will be linked, or offer a fundamental extension to, those that the company operates in. There will be other gaps too, in specific industry sectors or markets that will be changing due to regulations, economic factors or simply their own growth.

Competitors are another source of research. A great company will know who its competitors are, who its customers are and how they are performing. Research on the direction that they will be taking is another important area. They may be looking to diversify due to a client that they already service; this is something that the company could look to do as well, stopping them from gaining a stranglehold on that new area.

Becoming a niche or specialist business provider will provide additional revenue opportunities and give the company something new to offer. Looking internally at the services provided and the customer types that purchase them will identify whether there is a niche opportunity. Niches focus on a specific set of customers and can enable the company to achieve rapid growth in a market or industry.

Identifying a niche area then leads to further research to ensure that this is the best route for the company to trial. The buying criteria and requirements of this group of clients has to be established, and the company's expertise and track record in delivering products and services to these clients must be clearly demonstrable.

Look at the cost of entering this market: has that been prohibiting other players? There may be other economic or cultural reasons, but this could still be a game-changer if the company is cash rich and the forecasts are good.

Or the take-up may be too low. The market may need this product or service but cannot afford it or do not see the benefits clearly enough to purchase it. That could be simply a marketing issue, or it could be that the product is not actually worth enough to the niche market for them to want to buy it. There are lots of factors, but exploring them all means that sound decision-making takes place.

I have a client who operates in several large market areas within the automotive sector, where differentiation is difficult and identifying distinct groups of clients to target is also hard. They have recently decided to begin by honing in on one niche market and are focused on selling to a distinct set of clients who own single or fleets of heavy goods vehicles. They have not jumped straight in, but have researched their own customer base and looked at many other factors.

This will not be their sole market, but it will provide a very good specialist area for them to gain credibility and visibility in, which will in turn lead them to other clients, both within and outside the niche.

By identifying the buying chain that the company wants customers to travel along, products can be created that match every part of the chain, increasing in value and profit from a low starting point, towards the high value products and services representing the core business. The prospects can be very effectively targeted as a result.

Acquisitions and mergers also enable game-changing opportunities. Is there a part of the business, or even the whole company, that would benefit from being brought together with another player to increase market share and revenue, location growth or expansion?

The industrial relocation business I worked with had a specialist technical division that was in many ways not a natural fit with the overall company operation. They identified a competitor who had some key clients and several locations that would be very good for expansion.

The acquisition process went ahead, and was indeed a game-changing opportunity. The company was duly acquired and the newly merged operation was renamed and set up as a separate division, rather than remaining as a product within the company portfolio, having its own board, marketing and finance function.

This is a good example of how looking closely at the competition enabled the business to try something new and increase its market share while still retaining customer loyalty and a recognisable brand.

A merger can bring a similar result. If there is a player in the market who offers a complementary service to the same, or a different, customer base, there is an opportunity to join the two businesses together and gain both market share and an increase in revenues. This can also be a way of increasing the profile of the combined business in new markets, and in different geographical locations.

Businesses with different geographical locations can also enable each to gain more clients through already having a presence, introducing the other service offering and using it to leverage additional sales. Entrance into new countries will be easier where there is already an infrastructure and a sound business operating.

Technology can also play a big part in trying something new. Are there technologies that have been developed within the company that could be further developed or sold into other markets? If the technology has already been developed, the foundations are in place to package and sell it into other areas. If there is something unique that is already offered to customers, investigation into whether that process can be enhanced through the use of technology could also be a growth area.

Where will the new ideas position you? As an established company with a proven track record in the core business areas operated, there will already be an existing credibility. When looking at a game-change or trying something new, the additional market positioning that will be gained is important. It should not be detrimental to the established track record, but should be raising the profile in the right way for the company.

Where the company wants to position itself and and be seen by peers, prospective clients and existing clients is a very important part of the decision-making process for trying something new.

Internally, staff can be involved to look at new ideas. Different areas of the business can be tasked with looking for new opportunities as part of their objectives. They can narrow down these ideas and then debate and challenge to refine them, before presenting them.

Challenging staff to think of ideas based on their own areas of expertise can throw up some exciting thoughts. There will also be those ideas that will never work, are too costly to implement or simply not a good business decision however well presented and thought out.

However, if the 'ideas' section is made a formal part of the regular review process, it begins to encourage the team into actively looking for new ways to improve the business and increase revenues. This will lead to ideas that can be taken forward when considering a game-changer.

When the ideas are being challenged within the business, there are several factors that need to be considered. Firstly, does the idea fit with the company vision? A new product or service that does not meet the company's vision for itself and its growth will not be appropriate to develop.

Will the game-changer require a completely new client base? If it will, the cost of acquiring this needs to be taken into account. In addition, think about how this will affect the growth and retention of the current client base. Will the new client base be sustainable and willing to move away from their current suppliers in sufficient number to make the game-changer viable?

Sometimes the game-changer can complement the existing business, driving more revenue from an existing set of clients. These clients may be buying ad hoc or single services and are usually found at the higher value end of the company's sales chain.

The events company I worked in set up a mini production agency – effectively offering the same set of services as the core business, but packaged to meet the needs of high end clients and including the personal management of people who were seen within the industry as being specialists in their field. The production company could draw staff and resources from the main events company to service their client base, and the main business could pass them opportunities that called for a specialist team. This included producing and running the new collection shows for clothing companies, and showcasing new product lines for retailers.

This is a good example of trying something new: the agency was created to drive additional revenue streams and increase the level (and sophistication) of the services that we were providing. The agency contained staff who had previously been working in the main business, as well as introducing new specialist staff to boost the level of experience and to encourage additional customers.

The cost of entry was low as the infrastructure was already in place, and the premises we worked in had room for the new unit to be set up. There were minimal additional costs as the services and the majority of the personnel came from within the core business – effectively outsourced to the agency on demand.

There was a natural crossover point with some clients who were already employing us to carry out the higher level services, and these had to be managed carefully. More tender opportunities were sought to increase the agency client base, and a different approach was taken.

The company made use of existing products and services, leveraging them to create a game-changer without the need for huge capital investment.

Another example of trying something new and complementary to the current client base was a set of services that were easy to offer via telephone to top end corporate clients as an added value sale. Again, the infrastructure was already in place for this, as was the client base.

The issues were around how to provide these services on a 24-hour basis, without increasing the staffing costs in the UK. Our American operation held the key to this as they were already operating the service, and they needed a partner to provide the 12 hours of telephone cover that they were losing.

The additional cost of staffing through the night in the American operation made the service less financially viable in the short term, as the customer call patterns were not yet reliable enough to base a decision on. As they could not tell where they needed, or did not need, staff, they had to maintain a higher number of personnel for a time which had led to their interest in working with the UK.

A natural fit, with minimal investment needed, all it required was a software system to enable all staff involved to see each customer and the interaction that had taken place; a changeover briefing on any outstanding issues at the end of each shift; and a small amount of training in the UK for the staff who would be providing the services.

Once the ideas start generating, the finance team need to get involved. Ideally, they will be involved from the outset in the cross-functional work that has been put into place. Either way, they need to look at the viability of the ideas, the costs to bring them to market, the entry to market and also the time it will take for the investment to break even and start to pay back.

The game-changers need to be evaluated to see whether they will make a significant difference to the growth and performance of the company, both in the short term and in the long term.

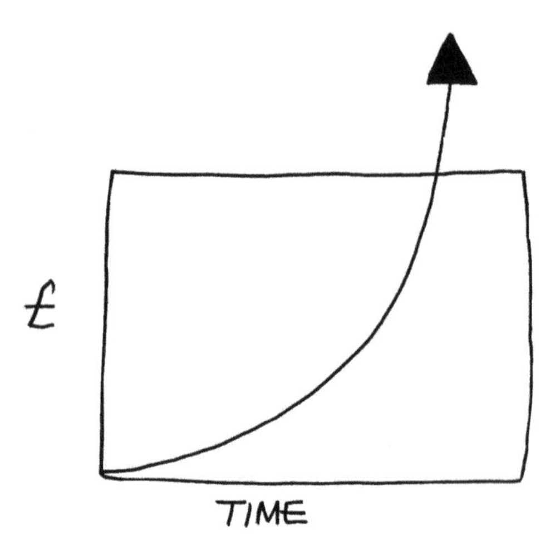

Challenging competitors will be a natural fallout of this process, and leading the way should be the desired outcome. Question whether the value perceived in trying something new is an internal value. It also needs to meet with external customer values too, and research with those prospective clients is another step in the process.

Buy in from the company

Generating ideas and plans for the game-changer should involve everyone. Ideas often come from unexpected sources or a chance conversation, and the more people in the company involved, the greater number of ideas generated.

This also ensures that everyone in the business is working together and can see transparently the ambition of the company to grow successfully. Explain why trying something new is important: it is not a threat to the current business and staff, but an opportunity for everyone to maintain their positions and be part of something new.

The growth of the company will mean an increase in revenue, an increase in success, and in turn will lead to promotional opportunities and additional jobs. Talented staff who have been identified will have something to embrace and will want to be part of the future success. Emergence of talent should also be an outcome of looking for something new to offer.

By looking at the team who work in the business, you will be able to identify those who need to be given an additional chance to improve their skills, or can give you the skills needed to make a game-changer work. It may not be personnel that senior management have a strong relationship with at the start, but there needs to be recognition that having the right people in place will drive the business forward – and this is the objective of identifying a game-changer.

It may be that some staff will need to be put onto a team through secondment, to explore and verify the ideas. In turn, this may create new positions and lead to a further opportunity to re-visit the previous staff structure and make some additional changes to benefit the core business.

Communicate well, throughout the whole company, in the way that is most appropriate to different staff at every level, and they will want to add their input and feedback. All feedback is good – often the critical feedback received will enable questions to be answered and therefore assists with the pitching process that will be needed to gain new clients.

Negative feedback enables the company to look at the idea and the 'why it will not work', putting together answers backed up with evidence, to overcome the objections. It is very good practice for questions that may be asked by prospective clients, chairpersons or stakeholders.

Some new potential products and services will not be relevant to everyone: there may be a patent issue or it may be a direct opponent to a competitor model for example. In these cases, I would still advocate communicating the general desire to generate new ideas and encourage everyone to be involved.

Explaining clearly a need for discretion around some announcements will lessen the Chinese whisper effect, the anxiety, and also the opportunity of scare-mongering amongst staff – which does and will always happen, no matter how great the company is and how hard it works to keep everyone involved and part of the process.

Testing it out

Research will be needed once you have identified one or more game-changing possibilities. The markets or industries that you are seeking entry to must be evaluated thoroughly to ensure that the game-changers have the maximum potential to succeed.

Establish whether there is a genuine market and client base for the products or services, or whether they are 'nice to have' but not true revenue growth drivers. If the offering is already in the marketplace, establish the points of differentiation between what the company is looking to provide and what already exists.

Where there is a perceived gap in the market, it is very important to ensure that research has been thoroughly carried out to make certain that the gap exists. Product or service names also need to be researched. Deciding on a name and then finding that it is already being used, whether in the market being entered or in a completely different one, can cause an unnecessary set back to a game-changer.

I work for a business that has developed a product for diesel engines and had already established their name and brand identity. By complete chance, a potential customer came across another company with a very similar name, purporting to offer a very similar product. This could have been disastrous for the company as the market they are entering is highly specialist and has several competitor products that it needed to differentiate and distance itself from.

Fortunately, we were able to decide on a different working name that would enable them to do this while still retaining the main elements of their brand identity.

Holding focus groups, or meeting with current clients and potential clients (where possible), for the new product or service is invaluable. Similar to gaining feedback within the company, these individuals will provide feedback from an external point of view, rounding off the research process.

Including objective voices from outside the company will also improve perception and positioning, and will create natural ambassadors and partners for the game-changer.

Establish the cost of creating a pilot model of the product or service – this should be part of the cost analysis carried out to identify the cost of market entry, and there should be a research cost allocated too.

A refined and more accurate picture of the cost of acquiring new clients should now be possible. This extensive research will also now provide the data to enable the company to decide on the nature and size that the game-changer will take.

One of the ways to test out a new product or service without committing to a full market launch is to find a potential client to pilot it. There are many benefits to doing this. By piloting the game-changer, valuable additional data and research can be undertaken in a test environment, allowing refinement and changes to be made before launch.

Another benefit of piloting is independent endorsement by a third party who is an industry expert in the area that the game-changer is being introduced. Independent endorsement can be used in marketing and sales materials, PR and advertising. It can also create potential customers who recognise the 'piloting' company and want to gain the same benefit for themselves.

Pilot testing will be the final piece of the process that leads to the decision of whether to launch the game-changer to fanfares and a blaze of publicity or whether to begin in a small niche market and build credibility and clients at a different rate.

If the game-changer is launched in a very visible way, the company needs to ensure that it is far enough ahead of its competition that they will not be able to overtake them whilst building credibility and a solid customer base. Again, this is where having a constant eye on competitor activity becomes very important. The company needs to know what stage they are at and whether they pose a risk – to either the introduction of the new product or service, and/or to the existing core business.

When a game-changer is launched using a low key method or almost as a 'cottage industry', it allows the product or service to continue being developed in one niche, with further pilot testing and refinement, which will lead to further independent endorsement.

It also allows the company to get the positioning of the game-changer defined and establish it slowly in one market or industry before moving on to the next one.

The company I work with that has developed the product for reducing fuel costs on diesel engines, has done exactly that. Their product has taken years of research and development – all carried out by the owners – before they looked for a pilot tester. The pilot testing has been running for a long time too, allowing them to make refinements and adjustments, and the company helping them has received significant benefit from the product at no cost.

The decision was made to grow in this way as they wanted to keep everything below the radar of some large players while they were getting the product completely finished and patented. They know that they have an amazing product that truly is a game-changer, but recognised that independent endorsement was the key to sales, rather than a large launch with no back-up testing.

The business is growing quickly now and has entered a new market – again using piloting and independent endorsement as the sales tool. They were already selling into the heavy goods vehicle market and are now selling their product into the commercial marine market. This is a good example of how making a smaller niche entry can have a greater long term effect on the production and growth of a game-changer.

You should develop a plan for continuous review in the testing stage. The product or service may need revisions, as may the delivery channel and many other aspects. It is important to have a budget for encountering issues and making the odd mistake; nothing is perfect from the beginning, and this is the reason for having the review and monitoring process.

If the new idea is not working, the thinking needs to be challenged and the game-changer may need to be adjusted. Good planning also includes the involvement of the 'objective voice' again, to make sure that the ideas and testing are being carried out thoroughly and remain relevant to both the market and the ethos of the company.

Finally, having a game-changer or trying something new will lead to increased credibility and visibility, but the process needs nurturing and will not produce results overnight. What it will do is to further encourage teamwork within the company, and give the company the right mindset for growth opportunities and changing the business.

Summary

- Look at what you already have in the company – can you create new opportunities from what exists?
- Can you identify a niche market to enter as a specialist?
- Think about a merger or acquisition
- Carefully consider the costs involved
- Carry out research and pilot testing

Summary

By taking all the steps I have suggested and discussed, your company will have built robust, fully tested plans that will enable you to move forward and grow successfully.

An improvement in staff involvement, succession planning and identifying emerging talent within the business will become obvious.

A far better understanding of who the customers are now, and what the target customers look like for the future ensures that marketing activity can be highly targeted towards the right companies and individuals and not just anybody.

Including an objective voice will make a big difference – challenge from someone outside but on the side of the company, ensures that the proposition going out to the market place has been challenged and is the best that it can be.

Making sure that marketing is happening throughout the business, and recognising that everyone – whatever their job role – is marketing the company every day, is crucial.

Acknowledgements

To the readers of my first draft for their comments and for taking the time out of their lives to help me, thank you! David Barrass, Sue Hurford, Chrissie Jenkins, John Lawson, Jennifer Priestley and Webster Springer.

To Lucy McCarraher at Rethink Press for her suggestions, which were invaluable.

Two significant others who have been a big part of my career: Elspeth Anderson for giving me opportunities I would not otherwise have had; and Evette Pottinger for being the best Marketing Executive anyone could wish for – keep shining, I am so proud of what you have achieved.

Clients who have trusted me with their business – thank you, I enjoy working with you all, it is a privilege.

The Author

Louise Walker has worked in many businesses over the past 20 years, holding senior corporate roles in several different disciplines before becoming a marketing director in an international events company.

In 2004, Louise formed her own marketing services company and specialises in working with business owners to create marketing strategies and plans, and also providing mentoring.

She is passionate about helping clients to increase their sales and delivering long term growth.

The experience she has gained working both in the corporate sector and in her own business forms the basis of this book, encouraging a fresh look at the marketing and strategy that is employed and making sure that it is embedded throughout a company.

Louise has developed her own Marketing Barometer. Her company, With Louise Walker Ltd, works with clients to identify and address their challenges and then create robust practical strategies that work.

Email hello@withlouisewalker.co.uk

Website www.withlouisewalker.co.uk

Lightning Source UK Ltd.
Milton Keynes UK
UKHW022209211119
353974UK00009B/590/P

9 781781 333891